⬤BENEVON™
MISSIONIZING YOUR SPECIAL EVENTS

How to Build a System of Events That
Engages Donors Who Will
Stay with You for Life

TERRY AXELROD

Missionizing Your Special Events—How to Build a System of Events That Engages Donors Who Will Stay with You for Life
Terry Axelrod

Benevon (formerly Raising More Money) Publications,
Seattle, Washington

The following trademarks appear throughout this book:
Benevon™, Point of Entry®, Next Step®,
Free Feel-Good Cultivation Event™, Cultivation Superhighway™,
Free One-Hour Ask Event™, Essential Story™, Visionary Leader™,
Emotional Hook™, Multiple-Year Giving Society™,
Units of Service™, Five-Step Follow-Up Call™.

All text and illustrations © in whole or in part 2008 Terry Axelrod.

Printed and bound in the United States of America. All rights reserved. No part of this book may be reproduced or transmitted in any form or by any means, electronic or mechanical, including photocopying, recording, or by an information storage and retrieval system—except by a reviewer who may quote brief passages in a review to be printed in a magazine, newspaper, or on the Web—without permission in writing from the publisher.
For information, please contact:
Benevon Publications, 2100 North Pacific Street, Seattle, WA 98103

Although the author and publisher have made every effort
to ensure the accuracy and completeness of information
contained in this book, we assume no responsibility
for errors, inaccuracies, omissions, or any inconsistencies herein.
Any slights of people, places, or organizations are unintentional.

First edition published in 2008.

ISBN: 978-0-9700455-9-1

The Library of Congress Cataloging-in-Publication Data
is available from the publisher.

ATTENTION CORPORATIONS, UNIVERSITIES,
COLLEGES, AND PROFESSIONAL ORGANIZATIONS:
Quantity discounts are available on bulk purchases of this book
for educational purposes. Special books or book excerpts can also be
created to fit specific needs. For information, please contact:
Benevon Publications, 2100 North Pacific Street, Seattle, WA 98103
Phone 888-322-9357

ACKNOWLEDGMENTS

Oddly enough, tampering with existing special events is sensitive business in the nonprofit world. Each event comes loaded with its own emotional and historical baggage and its band of fans or detractors. Therefore, my first thanks goes to each of the nonprofit organizations who are so fully engaged in our Curriculum for Sustainable Funding that they trust us and follow the Benevon Model. They have reaped the larger rewards that come from paring down all of the "fundraising fluff" to get to the basics of donor engagement and donor cultivation, ultimately leading to sustainable funding.

Next, thanks to our fine Benevon staff, senior management team, instructors, and coaches, who are so dedicated to the mission of every group we serve. They share in each group's angst in every way, including the grueling process of modifying or eliminating special events, and in the subsequent glee when the large gifts start coming in—all because the group stopped entertaining and started showcasing their real mission. Our coaches' adherence to the integrity of the model—in its purest sense—inspires me everyday.

Thanks to our great editorial and publications team—Ann Overton, Elizabeth Smith, Paulette Eickman, Miriam Lisco, and Melissa Lound—and especially to Lisa McCune, Benevon publications editor, for her sharp eye and skill in making this book a reality.

Finally, thanks to Bobbi Nodell, our brilliant former public relations specialist, who coined the word "missionizing" and the phrase "missionizing your events." Although we all know it's just a made-up term, it communicates!

Also by Terry Axelrod:

*Raising More Money—
A Step-by-Step Guide to Building Lifelong Donors*

*Raising More Money—
The Point of Entry Handbook*

*Raising More Money—
The Ask Event Handbook*

*Beyond the Ask Event—
Fully Integrating the Benevon Model*

The Joy of Fundraising

Videos by Terry Axelrod:

Introduction to Raising More Money

Re-Igniting Your Board

Seventeen Minutes to Sustainable Funding

TABLE OF CONTENTS

Preface vii

Chapter 1	Why Missionize?	1
Chapter 2	The Benevon Model	5
Chapter 3	Four Types of Events	21
Chapter 4	Soul-Searching Questions—Telling the Truth About Your Events	31
Chapter 5	The Classic Point of Entry Event	41
Chapter 6	Point of Entry Variations	63
Chapter 7	The Free One-Hour Ask Event	71
Chapter 8	Free Feel-Good Cultivation Events	83
Chapter 9	Point of Entry Conversion Events	95
Chapter 10	Post-Event Follow-Up	109
Chapter 11	Designing Your System of Events	117
Chapter 12	Milestone Events	133
Chapter 13	Making the Most of the Holiday Season	137
Chapter 14	Moving Forward	147

Appendix
   Visionary Leader Talk Worksheet 149
About the Author 151
Additional Information and Resources 153
Index 155

PREFACE

Events, special or otherwise, have become a staple of the fundraising diet of every nonprofit organization. From bake sales to black-tie galas, we all know what to expect when we show up: get out your checkbook and—in most cases—have fun! There's nothing wrong with that.

Somewhere along the line, good people who love the work being done by their favorite organizations got sidetracked into the entertainment business. They figured that, rather than having to talk to people about the amazing and meaningful work of their organization, if they could just entertain people—give them some good, honest fun or a product in exchange for their money—they'd have a winning fundraising event. The prevailing thinking was that people won't go for the serious stuff—they just want to have a nice night out, play some golf, and go home happy. So why get serious when we can just entertain people and get them to give money?

At Benevon, we say those days are over. While those events may raise short-term money—in many cases a lot of money—they generally are not designed to grow and develop the base of people who truly support the work of the organization. The value proposition is: we will give you an enjoyable evening, and in exchange, you will give us your money.

Think of the last fundraising event you attended. How did you get invited? Why did you say yes? How much did it cost you—when you add in the babysitter, the parking, and the new outfit you bought to look great there? What did you get in return? Did you have fun there? Would you have preferred to write the group a check and stay home? Did you learn anything memorable about the group putting on the event? The day after the event, could you have told someone the name of the group that benefited from your money and one inspiring thing about their work?

If you are a volunteer or on the board or staff of the nonprofit group that put on the event, was it really worth it? What did it build in the way of long-term support? Did you resent the amount of effort it took? At any point in the process, did you find yourself thinking, "There must be a better way than this to raise money"?

We have found, having worked with teams of board members, staff, and volunteers from more than 3,000 nonprofit organizations over the past twelve years, that it is time for that value proposition to change. People are hungry for more than a nice chicken dinner. If they are coming to an event anyway, why not educate and inspire them, so that in exchange for their ticket price, they can walk away knowing what their money might have helped your group accomplish—and a way for them to become more involved should they choose to do so?

The Benevon Model provides a template by which every nonprofit can convert its seemingly haphazard stream of labor-intensive events into a tightly crafted "System of Events." Over time, this system educates and inspires event guests and builds long-term relationships with major donors. As the organizations become more and more self-sustaining in their funding, they find that they are able to phase out many of their events.

And for groups that have very few special events, the model provides a blueprint for how to start from scratch and do it right—with as few events as possible!

In the chapters that follow, you will discover a new systematic approach for creating long-term sustainable funding for your organization from individual donors: the source of over 80% of the charitable funds contributed to nonprofits in America today.

Then you will learn to customize the ideal System of Events for your group. Be forewarned: this may be uncomfortable, as it will include how to strategically modify the program and format of each event, how to rotate the time of year of the event, how to substitute the event with a more program-related event, or how to eliminate an event altogether. Furthermore, in between each event, you will need to do a great deal of follow-up with guests.

This book is designed to restore the most important element in every event you ever put on from here on out—your organization's mission! And, in the process, you will learn to systematically connect with those special event guests to convert them into long-term supporters.

Ultimately, this book has one simple message: if your event is not, first and foremost, educating people about the real work of your organization in such a powerful way that they feel compelled to either become more involved with your organization or tell others about your work (or both), then you should not be having that event.

Conversely, if you take the time to carefully craft each event with a particular objective in mind, you can design a System of Events, and, over time, all of your events will integrate with one another to build long-term supporters who love your work and will engage others, not merely to sell a ticket or bring in short-term cash, but because they truly believe in the mission of your organization.

CHAPTER 1

WHY MISSIONIZE?

Unless your favorite nonprofit is the National Party Planning Society, odds are, your organization is feeling a bit guilty and off-purpose by being in the fundraising "entertainment" business.

Whether you provide direct services to children and families, advocacy, policy, or research, there is no doubt you started putting on fundraising events for the right reasons: to raise money for a good cause in exchange for people having a nice night out, a good day of golf, etc. In other words, you got into the "entertainment" business innocently, almost by default.

Somewhere, way back when (or even just last year), a well-intentioned person—often a revered board member—said what all good board members know to say when they hear yet again that the organization needs money: "Let's have a _____ event."

From that moment on, the scramble begins. The new event takes on a life of its own. The organization's limited resources shift away from other priorities in order to tackle this exciting venture: putting on the new special event that is going to save the day financially. Well-ingrained processes for budgeting and financial analysis are often cast aside in favor of the romanticism of the evening and the promise of the luscious bounty it will reap. Board members muster yet another round of energy to "tackle" their friends to join them at the latest and greatest new party. The event organizers work their tails off, and the event is hailed a success.

After the first event, people are abuzz. Regardless of its financial success, there is enough positive momentum and deference to the person who cooked up the idea that, *in the vacuum of no other permanent solution*, the event becomes an annual event by default. Not wanting to offend the board, staff members sit back and stoically add yet another event to their magical juggling act. The toll on staff is costly, and the turnover at these organizations is high.

Over the years, each nonprofit seems to acquire its own unique hodge-podge of these once-good-idea, party-style entertainment events, trapping the organization on that never-ending treadmill. Each event requires more staff and volunteers to fill tables, garner auction items, send out fancy invitations, and try to justify the flat or diminishing bottom line.

In the absence of a tested alternative to propose, no one is willing to do the simple financial analysis, taking into account the real costs of putting on the event, or to stand up to the board and say plainly, "This isn't working."

For most nonprofits, the special-events treadmill is an endless pathway and a distraction. Rather than these events being a means to an end (i.e., operational funding for a good cause), each event becomes an exhausting project in itself, trumping even the importance of the mission of the organization.

Until now, there has not been much of an alternative to suggest.

This book provides a highly successful, tested alternative—a template for a System of Events that can be customized to your favorite nonprofit organizations. This system has been tested over the last twelve years with more than 3,000 nonprofit organizations from the United States, Canada, and Europe that have participated in our Benevon Curriculum for Sustainable Funding. The curriculum is designed to build long-term relationships with individuals who will make larger and larger financial contributions to the work of your organization—not because they are getting a wonderful souvenir trinket, vacation, or bottle of wine in exchange, but because they truly *understand* the important mission of your group and choose to support it for the long term.

In other words, if you are going to invest your group's limited resources to put on these events, why not use your events strategically to grow relationships with people who could become long-term major donors?

Furthermore, why not use this as the opportunity to stop and clean house? Inventory that hodge-podge list of events still on the docket, and figure out how to either missionize them, tweak their format, move them to a different time of year so they accomplish a specific purpose within your System of Events, or eliminate them altogether. If you choose to adopt the Benevon Model for building sustainable funding, you may also want to add a limited number of new mission-focused events that will get the job done more efficiently.

In the chapters that follow, I will:

- Describe the Benevon Model for creating sustainable funding from individual donors.
- Delineate the four types of mission-focused events that build relationships with donors.
- Show you how to customize your own System of Events that will withstand the test of time.
- Help you get from here to there, evaluating:
  - The relevance of each event you are now offering.
  - Whether events should be kept, modified, rotated to a different time of year, or retired from your list of beloved events.
  - The need to add events in order to meet the requirements of the Benevon Model.

If you are willing to let go of the attachment to the special-events treadmill—planning event after event, desperately hoping to break even or exceed your financial goals each year—and take the necessary actions outlined in this book, you will end up with a short list of tightly crafted, highly intentional, mission-focused events, each with its own unique role to play in your System of Events.

This system will bring sanity and integrity to the process, all while showcasing the real star of the show—your organization's mission.

Let's move on to an overview of the Benevon Model.

CHAPTER 2

THE BENEVON MODEL

Let's start with basics—why are you doing all of this, anyway? Odds are, when it comes to the particular nonprofit you're involved with right now, you've become hooked! Whether its work is about teaching photography to urban kids, cleaning up beaches, or doing relief work in developing countries, there is something about the core mission of the organization that resonates with your personal mission and values. You want to see their work sustained. Perhaps you have recently joined the board or started volunteering. Maybe you've been around since the organization got started. Regardless, you are hooked.

What you really want for this group isn't another pretty party or wacky special fundraising event. What you want most is to see their mission fulfilled in the world. If you could just write them a check to cover the cost of that, you might consider doing so. Short of that, you would love to see them attain a high enough level of stability in their funding to ensure that they could be around forever.

We call that "sustainable funding."

All of our work at Benevon has been about giving nonprofits a roadmap to sustainable funding—a model that can be customized to each group's unique mission, structure, and culture so as to attract precisely the people who care deeply about the mission and are committed to sustaining the organization's work.

Ultimately, our model is designed to build endowments that will ensure the long-term viability of each organization that is willing to do the work to attain it, regardless of their size, location, or mission.

Our Benevon Model seems simple—a circular four-step process that systematically allows organizations to educate, inspire, connect, involve, and cultivate people who want to become more involved, then ask them to make significant multiple-year pledges for unrestricted operating funds and eventually for capital and endowment gifts. These satisfied, passionate donors, in turn, introduce others.

In application, the Benevon Model is quite complex. Our objective is not to apply a cookie-cutter approach to each organization. Rather, we work with each group to clearly define and quantify their definition of sustainable funding and to build a systematic plan for fulfilling on that goal, using each of the principles of our model. Over time, we train and coach each team of volunteers, board members, and staff to successfully attain that goal.

In the process, the culture of the organization shifts significantly. No matter how strong and confident (or weak and fragile) each group seems to be when we first meet them, by the time they leave our Curriculum for Sustainable Funding, they have shifted the prevalent conversation in their organization from scarcity and desperation to abundance and possibility. Their mission suddenly seems a lot more attainable to them. Rather than being burned out and frustrated from having to "strong-arm" their friends for money, board members and volunteers are satisfied and nurtured by their involvement. They have stepped off the fundraising treadmill once and for all.

Therefore, the next time a well-intentioned board member, volunteer, or staff member comes up with the next great idea for a special fundraising event (be it an "airplane pull" or a polo match), rather than everyone rolling their eyes and saying to themselves, "Here we go again," everyone on the team can say, "There's no need for any new events here—we already have a system that we're following, and it works!"

Please take the time now to read this brief summary of the Benevon Model. Even if you think you already know it, I will be referencing many of the terms used here as we go forward, and it will be important for you to understand the larger context for the events discussion that will follow.

The Benevon Model

IT'S A CIRCLE

The model is designed as a circle. Imagine a loop, a closed circuit, or an old-fashioned electric train set that goes around and around. Once your potential donors get on board, they stay on board. The cycle starts over each time they give. Your job is to tailor this model to your organization and to keep expanding it to include as many people as possible, year after year.

The model has four essential steps, which take you around the cycle.

Step One: The Point of Entry

Potential donors get on the track at a Point of Entry. The Benevon Point of Entry is a one-hour introductory event that educates and inspires people about your organization. You do not ask for money at a Point of Entry Event. You should assume that every potential donor will attend only one Point of Entry Event in their lifetime, so it should be memorable.

A Point of Entry Must Include Three Elements:
1. The basic information—the "Facts 101" about your organization, including the vision and needs.
2. An "Emotional Hook" so compelling that people will never forget it.
3. A system for "capturing the names," including addresses, phone numbers, and e-mail addresses of the guests, with their permission.

Your Point of Entry must give people a sense of how the work of your organization changes lives. This is because, as individuals, we are emotional donors looking for rational reasons to justify our emotional decision to give. Your Point of Entry Event must satisfy both the head and the heart; neither the emotion nor the facts alone will do it. The Point of Entry must intertwine myth-buster facts with heartfelt stories and a clear sense of the gap or current need. If you don't connect with both the guest's head and heart, you won't have a foundation from which to launch a relationship with a lifelong donor.

Finally, you must be sure you have a permission-based system to capture the names, addresses, phone numbers, and e-mail addresses of every guest. After all, if the Point of Entry Event is just the first point in a cycle of lifelong giving, you will need to know how to contact each person again. Rather than tricking or manipulating them by pretending to collect their business cards for some other purpose, you can ask people to fill out a card with their contact information because they have been told in advance what to expect. They know they are coming to a brief introductory session to learn about a wonderful organization. They know that they will not be asked to give money at the Point of Entry. They are coming because they have been invited personally by a friend or someone they trust.

When people are invited to your organization's Point of Entry Events, they are told the truth: that you are trying to spread the word about your work and solicit feedback about your programs from people in your community. After all, that is exactly what you are trying to do. However, the only way you will know what they really thought about your organization or your Point of Entry is if you ask them. Therefore, the second step on the circle is making a personal Follow-Up Call within a week to each person who attended the Point of Entry Event.

Step Two: Follow Up and Involve

If you are not planning on doing a rigorous job of following up with each and every person who attends a Point of Entry Event, there is no point in having these events at all. In fact, the very first step in planning each event should be to design your follow-up system.

The Benevon Five-Step Follow-Up Call is not a standard thank you, for which a note would suffice. It is an interactive research call. Think of it as a one-on-one focus group in which you gather critical data on each potential lifelong donor and friend. The purpose of this call is to generate an authentic dialog with true give-and-take. If you think of the people with whom you have lifelong relationships—your friends and family—you will realize that these relationships are rooted in a true dialog. It should be no different with your donors.

The Follow-Up Call must be made by someone your guests met at the Point of Entry, not by a stranger. This call follows a specific, five-point format that will help you get the information you need.

The Benevon Five-Step Follow-Up Call

1. "Thank you for coming." You certainly need to thank them. They are busy people who did not have to take the time to come to your Point of Entry.
2. Ask: "What did you think (of the tour, the organization, the issue)?" Ask enough questions to get them talking.
3. Listen. This is the hardest step for most of us, and by far the most critical component of the Follow-Up Call. Stop talking and listen. In this model, the more you listen, the more you will notice that potential donors are telling you exactly how they would like to become involved with your organization. If you are too busy talking or planning what you want to say next, you will miss all the rich cues.
4. If they have not already told you, ask: "Is there any way you could see yourself becoming involved with our organization?" You let them tell you. In the new reality of donor-centered individual giving, the donors have their own ideas—ideas that may not mesh with your needs. You still need to listen and be open to saying yes to what they offer.
5. Finally, ask: "Is there anyone else you think we should invite to a _____ (Point of Entry Event)?" You may be surprised to discover that, because people were truly inspired by your Point of Entry, they will naturally suggest others you should contact. Even people who are honest enough to tell you that your issue is not their top priority will have other people for you to invite. Ask if they would mind if you contact these people directly and use their name or if they would call the person first to tell them to expect your call.

Data Tracking

Every bit of data you gather must be recorded in your database. Be sure your computer system has a section for you to record notes about each contact with each donor and next steps.

Letting People Off the Hook: "Bless and Release"

In the follow-up process, you are sure to come across people who are not interested in getting more involved with your organization. The Follow-Up Call is where you can let them off the hook. Do not take this as a personal rejection or failure. Rather, put yourself in their shoes. They took the time to come to the Point of Entry. Yes, they were touched and impressed with what you do, but they are deeply involved in another cause that is their true passion. While they like you and know that you are doing good work, you are never going to make it to the top of their giving list.

Let these people go graciously. "Bless and release" them. Thank them sincerely for taking the time to attend your Point of Entry Event. If they are open enough to mention the other issue or organization they are involved with, compliment it. Honor their commitment and dedication to that cause. Do not offer to send them an envelope that they can use to make a small gift. *Let them completely off the hook.* It will disarm them and distinguish you from the others. Think of how grateful you would feel if people heard you the first time when you really meant "No."

In the long run, these people will help you in many ways, primarily by referring others. Many times, people have told me, "This type of program just isn't my thing. I'm deeply involved in another organization, and that's where I want to be putting my resources right now." Then, when I asked them the final question about others they know who might want to come to a Point of Entry, they would often say, "You should definitely call my wife (or my work colleague or my friend). This is exactly the kind of thing they'd be interested in. Tell them I recommend they come out and take your tour. In fact, I'll call them myself to tell them to expect your call." What better compliment than for a person to refer you to others and encourage you to use their name? In the long run, you will have made a real friend, just by letting someone off the hook.

Remember, this is a model for building lifelong donors—donors who are so interested in your mission that they want to stay with you for the long term. It is as if, one by one, you are selecting the people who are going to be part of your organization's family forever. You do not want to select someone who is not really interested. There are so many generous and caring individuals who truly understand and appreciate the value of what you are doing. They are the ones you are on a scouting mission to find.

The Cultivation Superhighway

Where we are headed in the model is along the path to the third step, where the donor will be asked for money. Notice you have not done that at either Step One, the Point of Entry, or at Step Two, Follow Up and Involve. You have been busy warming up and screening people to see if they would make loyal lifelong donors. In our model, by the time you get around to asking for money, you should be certain that the person is ready to give.

In the old reality, the "Ask" often happened too soon, before the person had a chance to fully buy in, head and heart, to the mission of the organization. In the new reality, there is no need for that. In fact, if you have any sense that the person may not be ready to give, don't ask yet. Trust your instincts and hold off until you know they are ready.

Asking is very much like picking the ripened, low-hanging fruit from a tree. When a person first comes to your Point of Entry, they are brand new to your organization, completely unripened fruit. By going through the tour, they begin to ripen, and with the Follow-Up Call, they ripen further. By the time you get around to asking them for money, it should be nothing more than "nudging the inevitable"—like easily picking a piece of fruit off a tree the moment it is ready. On the other hand, if you wait too long, what happens? The fruit becomes overripe, falls to the ground, and spoils. In other words, in the life cycle of each donor, there are perfect moments for asking for money. You have to tune your radar to those moments.

In this model, everything along the path between Step Two, Follow Up and Involve, and Step Three, the Ask, is called the Cultivation Superhighway. The more contacts you have with a potential donor along the Superhighway, the more money they will give you when you ask. There is a direct correlation between the number of contacts and the size of the gifts received.

This should come as no surprise. Again, think of yourself as that donor. Imagine that an organization had already taken the time to educate you and follow up personally. The more you heard from a real person at that organization directly and the more specifically their calls, e-mails, or meetings with you related to your particular needs, the more inclined you would be to give a larger gift the next time they asked.

It is worth considering what qualifies as a contact. Is it mailing a potential donor your newsletter or invitations to upcoming events? Yes, those do count as contacts, but nothing substitutes for a person-to-person, live contact. The best of these contacts are dictated by the donor. If they are generous enough in the Follow-Up Call to tell you how they might like to become more involved, your job is to stay in contact with them to make those things happen. Keep following up; keep giving them feedback.

If, for example, they would like to help you start a new program that you would love to have, you will need to invite them back to meet with the key staff in that area, the board, or the executive director. Or there may be other people from the community who the potential donor would also like to involve. Having them invite others to find out about your organization at a Point of Entry Event is also a key indicator of their support.

If you have done your homework and tended to their needs and interests throughout all of your contacts with them, this person will become a self-proclaimed volunteer for your organization. While their "project" may not fit into your normal job description for a volunteer, in the new reality of raising funds from individuals, this person is a volunteer with a customized, self-designed job description.

According to *Giving and Volunteering in the United States*, 84% of all charitable contributions come from households in which one or more family members volunteer. In other words, being a volunteer is a key indicator of giving. While the research doesn't specify that volunteers give to the same organizations where they volunteer their time, it does show that giving and involvement go hand-in-hand. And in the new reality of individual giving, you should assume that giving will follow involvement, in whatever way the donor defines involvement.

Donors need to know that you need them and that their contribution will make a difference in accomplishing your mission. They need to know that you are responsive to their suggestions. In many cases, they need to know that you need them for more than their money. For these reasons, the more meaningful your contacts are with these people, the better. Contacts are what ripen the fruit.

When the donor is ready to be asked, the first thing to consider is the medium you will use. Will you ask in-person, over the telephone, online, at an event, or by mail? Any of these is acceptable, although, generally speaking, the bigger the gift you are asking for, the more successful you will be if you ask face-to-face and one-on-one.

There are two ways to ask for money in our model, and most of our groups, over time, use both methods: asking one-on-one, in-person, and asking at the Free One-Hour Ask Event.

If you have taken many people through your Point of Entry Events in a short span of time, then followed up and involved them to their satisfaction, you may well find yourself in the enviable position of having a large number of people who are ready to be asked for a contribution at about the same time. In that case, the Benevon Free One-Hour Ask Event is ideal. The critical mass of true believers in the same room will produce remarkable results in just an hour.

Whether you are asking one-on-one or at the Ask Event, in our model, every Ask must include two essential ingredients.

Step Three: Asking for Money

Multiple-Year Pledges

The first essential ingredient in asking for money is that you ask people to become part of a Multiple-Year Giving Society by making a multiple-year pledge to support the unrestricted operating needs of the organization. That's right, you ask them to commit at the time of their first pledge to give that same amount each year for a specified number of years. Why? Not for the reason you may think. As wonderful as it is for your organization to know you have the stability of all those pledges waiting to be collected each year, that is not the main reason for asking for multiple-year pledges.

The main reason is for the donor. It allows donors to declare themselves as part of your organization's family. It gives a particular group of more committed donors the opportunity to say: "You can count on me. I'm a long-term believer in what you are up to."

Think for a moment about your own giving. Make a mental list of all the places you have been supporting over the years, getting relatively little feedback in return. Imagine that someone from one of those organizations called you and said, "We notice you have been a loyal donor for the last fifteen years. Thank you for your support. We are calling to ask if you would be willing to make a pledge to give at that same gift level for the next five years." You would have a hard time saying no, right? After all, you would probably keep giving there anyway.

The value of a Multiple-Year Giving Society is that it allows donors to "go public" with their commitment and support. Most of us are very private in our giving. We just keep sending in our little (or not so little) checks year after year. We are not looking for recognition. We each have our personal reasons for giving. We don't even talk about our giving with others. The satisfaction of giving is often more than enough.

Making a multiple-year pledge lets the organization know that we are deeply grateful for—and supportive of—their work. It gives us license to talk about our fondness for this organization with those close to us—the people we trust, respect, and confide in. Our natural tendency as people who have made that multiple-year commitment is to share our enthusiasm with others.

Units of Service

When asking for multiple-year pledges, it is crucial to specify the levels of contribution. We call these Units of Service. They are the giving levels or gift club levels—the bite-sized chunks of *unrestricted* funding that one person can support. They relate to the needs that were clearly identified at the Point of Entry and at every contact along the way.

If you are following the model, you will have three Units of Service, and there should be a significant gap in their dollar levels. The lowest level must be $1,000 a year (which equates to about $83 a month). Many people who truly love your work and want to be lifelong members of your organization's family can and will give at that level. In fact, many may already be giving at that level when you total up their multiple gifts each year.

The key thing to know is that these levels are made-up symbolic categories for funding the unrestricted operational needs of the organization, and in the new reality of lifelong donors, it is fine to tell people that. If they have bought into your mission fully, they will trust you to use the money for the overall programs of the organization. They know that someone has to pay the light bill and the salaries. They know they can look at your annual audit if they want to see exactly how the money was spent.

Step Four: Introducing Others; Reconnecting Existing Donors

In the fourth step of the model, each individual member of the Multiple-Year Giving Society receives a Follow-Up Call to thank them for their gifts and pledges and to ask them to introduce others to your organization by inviting their friends and associates to Point of Entry Events. Since your donors have been treated well as they have gone around the cycle with you, they know you will take good care of their friends. You will educate and inspire them at the Point of Entry, follow up personally, involve them as appropriate, or "bless and release" them if they are not interested. Your Multiple-Year Giving Society Donors will trust the organization to treat their friends with respect. Their secret hope, of course, is that their friends will fall in love with your organization too—in their own right, for their own reasons—and become lifelong donors as well. This step completes the first circuit around the model for a brand-new donor.

Free Feel-Good Cultivation Events: Points of Re-Entry

To keep your donors in the cycle, every Multiple-Year Giving Society Donor is invited to one or two Free Feel-Good Cultivation Events during the year—also called Point of Re-Entry Events. These program-related events serve to reconnect them to the emotional impact and the facts about your work. Donors are encouraged to invite others to Free Feel-Good Cultivation/Point of Re-Entry Events. For these new guests, this event will be their Pre-Point of Entry. For the prior donors, the event serves to reinforce their wise investment in your organization and to deepen their interest and commitment.

These Free Feel-Good Cultivation Events can be regularly scheduled events having to do with the work of the organization, such as a graduation of your program's participants or a lecture on a topic of interest, or they can be events planned specially for these donors. You may even choose to have different events for donors at different levels.

Following each Free Feel-Good Cultivation Event, every donor receives another one-on-one Follow-Up Call asking a few more open-ended questions and giving the donor the opportunity to offer suggestions for names of others to be invited to a Point of Entry. This in turn leads to more cultivation, more involvement, and deeper permission and trust. Whatever they tell you in each Follow-Up Call determines the frequency and quality of involvement this particular donor would like to have, including the timing of the next Ask.

After the next gift is received, another Follow-Up Call is made to say thank you, there is more conversation, and on it goes. All the while, you are looking and listening for how else they might want to become involved. You may even consider inviting them to take on a leadership role in a key volunteer or board position, as appropriate.

Ideally, in the course of the year, you will have three or four occasions for personal, one-on-one contact with each donor. This contact can be made by your lead development staff person, other key staff, or by one of your volunteer donor service representatives (akin to a customer service representative in a bank) who is assigned to that donor for at least two years at a time. These contacts are nothing intrusive or artificial, but rather a natural give-and-take, either triggered by gifts received or by their participation in one of your Free Feel-Good Cultivation Events.

Growing the Model to Sustainable Funding

The Benevon Model is designed to attain sustainable funding. Each nonprofit may define that differently. We define it simply as an endowment fund large enough to generate sufficient earnings to cover the annual fundraising needs. Many groups prefer not to have an endowment. Rather, they define sustainable funding as a reserve fund of a specific size or a minimum number of new major donors or amount of funds raised each year.

By using the model systematically over time, this simple circle becomes a spiral, with an ever-growing number of Multiple-Year Giving Society Donors. When cultivated personally, using our specific guidelines for cultivation, many of these same donors will give generously for other needs of the organization, including capital campaigns, endowment, and restricted major gifts, such as for a research project or special program fund.

The model provides a natural mechanism for attracting and involving new people, while regularly "blessing and releasing" those who choose not to become involved, and systematically cultivating those who have both the passion for the mission and the resources to become major donors.

Let's move on to the four types of events in the Benevon Model.

CHAPTER 3

FOUR TYPES OF EVENTS

Now that you have an overview of the Benevon Model, you might already be thinking about how you could convert many of your more labor-intensive, stand-alone special events into events that can advance your system for building sustainable funding from lifelong donors.

Before we can delve into how to missionize each of your existing events, we need to step back and review the Benevon classification of events.

In this model, any event your organization is now putting on can be recast to fit into one of the following categories:
1. The classic Point of Entry and its three derivative events:
   - The Point of Entry in a Box
   - The One-on-One Point of Entry
   - The Pre-Point of Entry
2. The Free One-Hour Ask Event
3. The Free Feel-Good Cultivation Event
4. The Point of Entry Conversion Event

As we go through these descriptions, notice the elements that are common to each event. There is one similar theme to them all: your organization's mission! Each event includes facts, emotion, and capturing the names of the interested guests with their permission. Each event is followed by a personal Follow-Up Call to ask for the person's feedback about the event and their level of interest in moving forward with you.

THE CLASSIC POINT OF ENTRY

The cornerstone of the Benevon Model, this free, one-hour, get-acquainted event educates and inspires people about your mission. People are invited word-of-mouth by a friend to a small gathering of ten to fifteen people where they are educated and inspired about the real work of your organization. They are told in the invitation process that you want them to come and learn about the work of the organization and that you will be asking them for their feedback on the program after the event. They are told in advance that they will not be asked for money. These events are held at least once a month, rain or shine, all year long.

The carefully crafted, high-touch, low-tech program, which includes a greeting from a board member, a Visionary Leader Talk, and a tour filled with myth-buster facts and succinct, powerful stories and testimonials, moves guests to tears and leaves them wanting to get on the phone to tell people what they just saw and learned. It should be a life-changing event for each guest, whether or not they choose to become more involved with your group.

The Point of Entry in a Box

Once your Point of Entry format is tested and refined over time, it becomes so repeatable that you could almost put it in a box (except for the people, of course) and take it on the road. At that point, your organization can also begin offering what we refer to as Point of Entry Events in a Box, which can be held in your board members' conference rooms, volunteers' living rooms, church halls, etc. Although you will still need to take the other speakers with you, the Point of Entry in a Box opens up many other venues and times of day to reach more people with your message.

While board members and volunteers may host these events or invite people to them, the majority of the new Point of Entry guests are referred by prior Point of Entry guests. At least 25% of guests should be referring others—otherwise your Point of Entry isn't sizzling enough!

The One-on-One Point of Entry

Eventually your group will become comfortable with the Point of Entry process, and people will realize that many of the elements of the Point of Entry could be consolidated into a One-on-One Point of Entry. Although this is not a substitute for a real Point of Entry, the story telling, the facts, and the compelling vision for the future can all be conveyed in a dialog between two people over the holiday punchbowl, sitting on an airplane, or standing in line at the bank. Suddenly each of your volunteers becomes a powerful ambassador for your work, spreading the word out in the community, and generating more guests for your Point of Entry Events.

The Pre-Point of Entry

A first cousin to the classic Point of Entry is the Pre-Point of Entry. This category is not actually part of the Benevon Model, but I have made a placeholder for it here because so many people ask us what to call those events like civic club presentations, Rotary meetings, public information sessions, nonprofit fairs at a shopping mall, etc. At these events, the "guests" are not necessarily expecting any particular presentation from your group, nor would it be appropriate to contact each person afterwards, since they have not given express permission for you to do so.

People who give you a card at the end of your presentation at the Rotary meeting or people who express interest at a "booth-style" type of fair cannot be considered to have attended a Point of Entry. However, if they give you their card or request a personal follow-up, you then have their permission to do a formal Follow-Up Call and invite them to come to your regularly scheduled Point of Entry.

Another example of a Pre-Point of Entry is a story told by our gifted senior instructor, Lynda Bowman. While Lynda was dropping off used household items at the curb of a local domestic violence shelter, the young man who took away her bagged items asked if she would like to attend one of the upcoming tours of the shelter and gave her a flyer with the date and details of their next Point of Entry.

While these public events can be very time consuming and may seem "unproductive" in terms of generating more Point of Entry guests and advancing your success in building sustainable funding, they can be wonderful public relations activities, and we certainly encourage our groups to participate in them if they can honestly find the time to prepare and attend.

Passion is the Key

Whichever Point of Entry or Pre-Point of Entry a guest first attends, they get a firsthand experience of your mission and your passion for the work of the organization. The people inviting their friends are passionate about your work. The people speaking at the Point of Entry are passionate. The stories about the people whose lives are changed by your work evoke more passion, inspiring the guests to introduce others. There is nothing phony or inauthentic about the process. It isn't a sales pitch. It rings true all the way through.

Within one week of attending the Point of Entry, each guest who has given you permission to contact them receives a special Follow-Up Call, asking key questions to discern their level of interest in moving forward with you. Listen closely to "bless and release" those people who do not want more contact, but not before asking them if there is anyone else they can think of who you should invite to an upcoming Point of Entry. Many will have referrals for you because they were truly touched by your Point of Entry.

THE FREE ONE-HOUR ASK EVENT

The second event is the Benevon Free One-Hour Ask Event. While other special events may resemble this, it is unlikely that they are identical to this event. Many aspects of the event are counterintuitive and can be done properly only in conjunction with the rest of the model. In other words, it is not a stand-alone event.

To qualify as a Free One-Hour Ask Event in this model, at least 40% of the guests must have attended a Point of Entry in the prior year. Each guest is personally invited to a free breakfast or lunch event by a friend who serves as a Table Captain. The Table Captain tells them that they *will be asked to give money* at the event, but there is "no minimum and no maximum gift" expected. As much as anything, they are being asked to come and learn more about the organization. It will be the organization's job to inspire and educate them so they will want to give.

The Ask Event provides a straightforward, time-limited immersion into the outstanding work of your organization. In one tightly choreographed hour, this event provides the Facts 101, the Emotional Hook, and a compelling Ask for multiple-year support at specific giving levels.

This event is an extremely effective fundraiser for the following reasons:

1. A minimum of 40% of the guests have already been personally involved by attending a Point of Entry and receiving a Follow-Up Call and several subsequent contacts. They serve as a critical mass within the larger group and will be the primary givers at the event.

2. The guests have been well prepared in advance and know that making a contribution will be optional at the event. You should expect that no more than half of the people will give at all on the day of the event. That is because the "pitch" is delivered in a clear, low-pressure way.

    The people who have already come through your Point of Entry Events and have become more involved through the cultivation process will be ready to give. These people give at least four times more than the other people who give. The majority of the people who have not been to a prior Point of Entry will not give at all on the day of the event. Many will want to come to a "real" Point of Entry. About 55% of the guests should give nothing at all.

3. The event is free. In fundraising, "free" is magical. If you were to charge even $10 per person to attend this event, it would never be as successful. At a Benevon Ask Event, people are given a basic breakfast or lunch, for which they do not feel overly obligated. They are free to enjoy themselves and to give when asked, if they so choose. Do not do this event as a

dinner. Dinner cannot be accomplished in an hour, and dinner implies a greater degree of obligation, which has proven to get in the way of donors choosing how much they would like to give.

Note again that the Ask Event includes the same critical elements as the other events: the Facts 101, the Emotional Hook, and capturing the names with permission. And, again, just like after the other events, Follow-Up Calls are made right after the Ask Event, but not to everyone who attends—only to donors and Table Captains.

THE FREE FEEL-GOOD CULTIVATION EVENT (Also Known as the Point of Re-Entry Event)

The third type of event in the Benevon Model is the Free Feel-Good Cultivation Event. The name pretty much says it all. These are the "reward" events for your Multiple-Year Giving Society Donors that reconnect them to the Emotional Hook and reinforce the wisdom of their investment in your organization. That means these events *always* include a program or theme that ties to your mission.

Do not underestimate the magic of a "free" event. If you inspire them, people will remember you gave them something for free when it comes time to ask them for the next contribution. Just make sure you have one or more underwriters who receive plenty of credit, so your loyal donors will know you did not spend any of their money to pay for this event.

The best Free Feel-Good Cultivation Events are internal program-related events, already planned, to honor your clients or families, such as graduations, show-and-tell nights, special theater performances, expert lectures, etc.

Free Feel-Good Cultivation Events are not designed to attract new friends to the organization, but rather to cultivate your inner circle of Multiple-Year Giving Society Donors. Of course, these insiders are always encouraged to bring friends to the Free Feel-

Good Cultivation Events as well, so long as the focus of the event really is on your loyal prior donors. (For the new people, the event will serve as a Pre-Point of Entry Event. Just be sure to do the same rigorous follow-up work with them that normally follows a Point of Entry Event.)

Free Feel-Good Cultivation Events can take many forms. First and most obvious are the traditional recognition events, such as awards dinners or dinner parties in private homes, so long as they include a program with facts and emotion.

In a second category are the informal, but invitation-only, in-house, program-related events, such as a special night for donors to serve soup in your soup kitchen or a special pre-graduation reception for Multiple-Year Giving Society Donors.

In the third category are the formal or informal briefings or updates with a celebrity scientist or artist on their newest work or discovery.

These events can also be varied for donors at different giving levels. You may invite your biggest donors to an elegant dinner at the most exclusive private home with your CEO or a revered person in your field, if that is something they would enjoy. Your other Multiple-Year Giving Society Donors might be invited to a dinner or lecture series, a family picnic, or a special "environmental day" or "peace day."

Free Feel-Good Cultivation Events may also be used to introduce insiders to the next dream for the organization, especially a campaign for capital, major gifts, or endowment.

This event clearly includes the critical elements of the Facts 101 and the Emotional Hook, and capturing the names is usually not necessary because you already have the names of all the donors in attendance. After all, you invited them to the event!

Finally, just as with a Point of Entry Event and each of the other events, a Free Feel-Good Cultivation Event always engenders a Follow-Up Call, eliciting more feedback, which in turn enables you to further customize your approach to each donor. This keeps the donor going around the cycle with you.

Planning Your Free Feel-Good Cultivation Events Strategically

I recommend a minimum of two Free Feel-Good Cultivation Events per year—one targeted to your highest Multiple-Year Giving Society Donors and one for all of your Multiple-Year Giving Society Donors. Ideally, you should also have a third event for all of your donors (including those not in your Multiple-Year Giving Society).

As for the best times of year to hold these events, they are most often scheduled to occur about three months after your Ask Event and three months before your next Ask Event. Ideally, these will coincide with natural program events such as arts performances, graduations, and holiday celebrations.

POINT OF ENTRY CONVERSION EVENTS

The fourth type of event is what we call a Point of Entry Conversion Event—the traditional fundraising event, like the gala or golf tournament, which we modify to fit into the model. *These events are not required at all in the model.* In fact, your goal should be to phase out as many of these events as possible, rather than converting them. Technically, these events should be considered Pre-Point of Entry Events, but we give them a category of their own to mark them as distinct for the many groups who, when they first begin implementing the Benevon Model, are so heavily dependent on the funds that they derive from these events and are reluctant to eliminate them immediately. As an interim solution, by inserting a well-crafted, brief, mission-focused element into the program and capturing the names of the people interested in learning more, that traditional, entertainment-style event can lead to follow-up and cultivation of a small segment of guests, who can then be invited to a "real" Point of Entry.

Having said that, converting a traditional fundraising event into a Point of Entry Conversion Event is still not nearly as efficient as inviting people to your real Point of Entry Events, where they will know what they have been invited to, the entire program will be about your mission, and you will have permission to follow up with everyone.

Assuming there are some events you feel you must keep, at least for the next year, here is a simple test to see if you have successfully converted each event to a Point of Entry Conversion Event: the next day, if someone were to ask your guests about the dinner-dance or the golf tournament, could the guests have answered the following two-question pop quiz?

Question 1: What was the name of the organization for which the event was raising funds?
While they may well remember how much they enjoyed the golf or the dinner-dance, will they be able to recall the name of the organization that worked so hard to produce the event and ultimately received their financial support?

Question 2: What does that organization do?
Even if your name is well known in your community, do not assume that people truly know about the breadth of your programs. What people will remember most is a short testimonial from someone who has benefited from your work.

In other words, you will need to insert a Point of Entry element into the sit-down portion of your fundraising event. This should include a short Visionary Leader Talk with facts and emotion, plus a brief, live testimonial from a person whose life has been changed thanks to the work of your organization. With good preparation, this can all be accomplished in ten minutes.

Capturing the names with permission in order to make Follow-Up Calls is a bit trickier, since people did not know in advance that they would be asked to receive a Follow-Up Call. You cannot assume that just because you have the name and contact information for each guest, you have their permission to contact them. Rather, you must secure their explicit permission to be contacted at some point during the event.

The easiest way to do this is by placing a card under their lunch or dinner plate or in the center of their table. The emcee needs to refer to the card and encourage people to fill it out and leave it with their table host if they would like to speak directly with someone from the organization.

Again, you can see that the Point of Entry Conversion Event must include the same critical elements as the Point of Entry; namely, it must include the Facts 101, the Emotional Hook, and a mechanism for capturing the names of the guests with their permission. Finally, you must plan in advance when you will be making the Follow-Up Calls after these events.

DESIGNING YOUR SYSTEM OF EVENTS

Now that you understand the event classifications within the Benevon Model, you are ready to begin designing your System of Events—a lasting set of events that build on each other throughout the year, providing each donor or potential donor with precisely the number and quality of contacts they would like.

For starters, I recommend the following:
- One Point of Entry Event per month.
- One Free One-Hour Ask Event per year.
- Two or three Free Feel-Good Cultivation Events per year (one for your highest Multiple-Year Giving Society Donors, one for all Multiple-Year Giving Society Donors, and the other for all of your donors).
- As few Point of Entry Conversion Events as possible—ideally, none at all.

If you do not already have any "fundraisers," we do not encourage you to add them. The next chapter will ask some "soul-searching questions" to help you decide whether or not to keep your existing fundraising events, which are usually very time-consuming.

CHAPTER 4

SOUL-SEARCHING QUESTIONS —TELLING THE TRUTH ABOUT YOUR EVENTS

As you become more familiar with the Benevon Model, you will likely come to regard your existing special events in a new light. You will either see them as wonderful occasions to introduce or further cultivate donors, or as events that have served their useful life and need to be "blessed and released."

In other words, it is time to put each of your existing events under the microscope and evaluate its role moving forward. Ultimately, if you choose to keep an event, it needs to have a very clear purpose and timeline, including a process for evaluating its efficacy each year so that it doesn't become unnecessarily entrenched.

LIST YOUR EVENTS

Start by making as broad of a list as possible of all the events your organization currently puts on each year. Include all types of events: annual dinners, holiday parties, volunteer and donor recognition events, anniversary events, golf tournaments, walk-a-thons, theater events, black-tie galas, auctions, etc. You can even include volunteer-recruitment events, training classes, or actual performances of your arts organization.

SYSTEM OF EVENTS

Current Events	Convert Event To:						Ideal Month	Add/ Convert/ Eliminate By When
	Pre-Point of Entry Event	Point of Entry Event	Point of Entry in a Box	One-on-One Point of Entry	Point of Entry Conversion Event	Free Feel-Good Cultivation Event		
1.								
2.								
3.								
4.								
5.								
6.								
7.								
8.								
9.								
10.								

SOUL-SEARCHING QUESTIONS

Right now, while you are alone reading this, without your staff, board, or event committee at your side, take the time to answer these questions honestly for each of the events your organization currently produces.

1. Why are you really having the event, anyway?
2. Is there really an expectation that this event will raise money?
3. What have you said in the past to justify not reaching your dollar goal for this event?
4. How attached are you and your organization to this type of event?
5. What if someone just walked in and wrote you a check for your total goal? Would you still have the event?
6. Thinking ahead to your next big event, if you don't make your goal, what will be the reason?
7. If the event is supposed to be a fundraiser, do you know how much it actually nets?
8. How many volunteers did it really take to put the event on?
9. If you have a dedicated fundraising staff, what else could they have been doing with the same amount of time and energy to bring in more money than the event nets?
10. For how many months in advance have you and your team been obsessing about the event?
11. Do you know from the beginning that you have big fixed costs to meet?
12. Is this the right kind of event for your organization?
13. Does this type of event give you enough predictors of the results?
14. Is this event the best way to maximize the giving potential of each donor?
15. What would you think if you had to sit through that program?
16. What are you building for future years by having this event?
17. On a scale of one to ten, how excited are you about producing this event?

Now that you've had the opportunity to answer these questions, let's look a little deeper at each soul-searching question.

1. *Why are you really having the event, anyway?*
   Don't be surprised if you don't really know or if there is more than one reason. Often, there is one "official" reason you tell the public. For example, to raise money for scholarships, to send more kids to camp, to honor the retiring founder or a visiting dignitary, etc. And then there is the real internal reason for having this event. Perhaps it is to please a particular person on the board or a key volunteer who loves planning this party every year. Or maybe it is just because you have been having the event for twenty-five years and no one would dare to stop it now.

2. *Is there really an expectation that this event will raise money?*
   Is there actually a stated fundraising goal for the event and, if so, is this goal different from the amount you absolutely must raise to fill a budget gap? Is someone having sleepless nights about needing this money to offset other funding cutbacks? Is everyone really expecting the event to raise the budgeted amount, or is that number inflated or underestimated? Conversely, is the goal too low and too easily attainable? What amount would you be thrilled to raise?

3. *What have you said in the past to justify not reaching your dollar goal for this event?*
   Do any of the following statements sound familiar?
   - "At least we made the board and volunteers happy."
   - "We had no other choice; everyone expects us to put on this event. It's an annual tradition."
   - "It's an opportunity to get our name out there in the community."
   - "It lets us tell our story to a broader group of people."
   - "It's a 'friend' raiser."

Most of the time, these kinds of statements justify the fact that, despite your best efforts, you don't know how to have the event make more money, which is not a good sign for next year's results.

4. *How attached are you and your organization to this type of event?* How attached are the others who are involved? Do they know the facts about how little it nets for the amount of work it takes to produce? Often, groups hesitate to eliminate an event for fear of losing a key volunteer leader associated with the event. When groups take the time to explain the costs and benefits of putting on the event, they are often surprised to find that those volunteers have come to feel burdened by the event and welcome the opportunity to phase it out or blend it into another event.

5. *What if someone just walked in and wrote you a check for your total goal? Would you still have the event?*
This is the real "moment of truth" question for most groups. They know right away as they look through their long lists of events, which ones are still worth keeping in spite of the work, and which ones need to be phased out, quickly or gradually. Pretend for a moment that you alone had the power to eliminate each event. If you knew you had the monetary goal covered, which events would you get rid of? Which events are the most difficult and annoying?

6. *Thinking ahead to your next big event, if you don't make your goal, what will be the reason?*
    - "We didn't start early enough."
    - "The board didn't do its job and sell enough tickets."
    - "The weather."

    It is interesting to notice that you probably already know what the reasons and excuses will be, yet you continue to go through the motions.

7. *If the event is supposed to be a fundraiser, do you know how much it actually nets?*
Has anyone actually calculated the true costs, adding in all the staff costs in addition to volunteer time and the obvious hard costs? While no smart board member would ever run a business this way, somehow when it comes to special nonprofit fundraising events, everyone just trusts that someone else has already figured out that the event will raise a lot of money.

8. *How many volunteers did it really take to put the event on?*
Did the event burn them out or make them happy? Are they bored with the event? Would they rather have hosted a smaller gathering where the Visionary Leader and a Testimonial Speaker could come and tell their story?

9. *If you have a dedicated fundraising staff, what else could they have been doing with the same amount of time and energy to bring in more money than the event nets?*
This is another zinger. While the event may seem like a good use of staff time, consider the distraction factor and the opportunity cost—the number of hours the staff could not devote to major-donor cultivation and asking. What might that have yielded?

10. *For how many months in advance have you and your team been obsessing about the event?*
What about the terror of the weeks and days before the event approaches, or the fear of whether you will even make the break-even number, assuming you know what that number is? Trust that "terror factor" as soon as you feel it. Too often, we see groups overriding their instincts telling them to cancel an event, numbly marching past the point of no return and having big regrets later.

11. *Do you know from the beginning that you have big fixed costs to meet?*
    These are things like theater ticket sales, pricey food costs, audio/visual equipment, room rental costs—anything you couldn't get donated. Beware of these high break-even events. Most nonprofits are unsophisticated in the world of venue procurement and black-tie dinners. It is very easy to get in over your head, where all potential "profit" from the event ends up covering unnecessarily high fixed costs.

12. *Is this the right kind of event for your organization?*
    Is it consistent with your mission? How could it showcase your mission even more? Is it the best way to tell your organization's story? We had one group that served homeless families. Their big fundraiser was a home tour of the fanciest homes in town. Another Christian group had a Bingo party as their big fundraiser. If you must take on these entertainment-style events, at least be sure they are sending the right message to your community and supporters!

13. *Does this type of event give you enough predictors of the results?*
    Are there enough benchmarks along the way to let you adjust accordingly in advance if you have fewer Table Captains or tickets sold? Usually there are many such checkpoints. If it's an all-or-nothing risk, you should back away from it.

14. *Is this event the best way to maximize the giving potential of each donor?*
    Proud as you may be for having gotten that big corporate sponsor to give you $1,000 to $5,000, consider how much more you might have gotten had you done the cultivation work to request a larger gift. What about the risk of several of your volunteers asking the same corporation for a gift, thereby confusing them and again getting you less than the ultimate gift?

15. *What would you think if you had to sit through that program?*
    Do people really care about the speaker? Is the speaker's message even relevant to your organization, or is the speaker just there to draw in more guests? If the latter, then how many more people will that speaker attract? How much more in the bottom line? Will that extra revenue more than cover the speaker's fees? What is the likelihood those guests who come just to hear this speaker will ever become lifelong donors? Would guests have preferred to just give you a check and skip the event altogether? More and more, we are hearing from donors, "Do I really have to go to another event?" The more they are connected to your mission, the less you will have to entertain them.

16. *What are you building for future years by having this event?*
    Where does this event fit into your overall individual giving program? Does it help you access a new group of people who give you permission to follow up with them? Does it allow you to acknowledge existing donors? Or is its purpose strictly to raise short-term money in an entertainment setting?

17. *On a scale of one to ten, how excited are you about producing this event?*
    You will need to be the cheerleader in those inevitable stressful days between now and event day. Your enthusiasm and commitment to the success of the event will be needed to carry the team forward. If you are not truly excited about what this event will accomplish for your organization, it may be time to speak up now.

If you have taken the time to tell the truth about each of your events, you should have a good sense of which ones you are committed to keeping and which ones should be converted or dropped.

GETTING FROM HERE TO THERE

Now that you understand the basics of the Benevon Model, the four types of events, the components of an ideal System of Events, and the soul-searching questions to ask about each event, we are ready to begin the process of "missionizing" each of the events that you plan to keep and crafting a System of Events that will tie it all together.

Each of the next five chapters will give an in-depth description of how each type of event works, how to convert other events into mission-focused events, and examples of types of events that can be successfully converted. Please do not jump to conclusions about which events you should convert yours to. There are many subtleties that will seem counterintuitive, so please read all five chapters to understand the rationale behind each. As we tell our groups, *the number one pitfall with the Benevon Model is getting creative with the formulas and the process*. It is all laid out here for you to follow.

CHAPTER 5

THE CLASSIC POINT OF ENTRY EVENT

The cornerstone event in the Benevon Model is the classic Point of Entry. This highly engaging, one-hour, get-acquainted event is definitely the event to zero in on if you are just getting started with the Benevon Model.

Since most groups are not doing what we would consider a true Point of Entry, you will likely need to develop a generic, sizzling Point of Entry that you and your team will love. In other words, this is an event that you will need to add. This chapter will help you design your Point of Entry Event.

For a detailed step-by-step guide to designing the ideal Point of Entry for your organization, including scripts, templates, and many sample Point of Entry formats, I would recommend you read *Raising More Money—The Point of Entry Handbook*.

The purpose of the Point of Entry Event is to educate and inspire people, not to ask for their money. The Point of Entry casts the net widely into the whole community by friends inviting friends to come to an informational session about your organization. The passion of the people who are inviting their friends is what will get people to attend. Once they arrive, you have sixty minutes to engage them in the facts and emotional impact of your work, leaving them so inspired that, as they leave, they can't help but get on their cell phones to call a friend or colleague to say, "You've got to see what I just saw. You've got to come to one of these events to learn about this great organization." Friends won't refer friends to something that's just mediocre, so you've got to make your Point of Entry really memorable.

Eventually, after refining and testing your basic Point of Entry, the content and format will become so generic, it's as if you could put it all in a box and take it to someone's home or office, in addition to presenting it at your own site—a Point of Entry in a Box.

Here are the technical requirements for a classic Point of Entry:

1. It lasts for one hour or less.
2. It takes place once a month, at a minimum.
3. No one is asked for money—either directly or indirectly.
4. Guests are asked to attend through a word-of-mouth invitation, preferably by a friend.
5. The event gives guests a "sizzling" experience of your mission—some would say it is "life changing."
6. At least 25% of the guests who attend your Point of Entry Events refer others to attend subsequent Point of Entry Events. This is the only true measure of a "sizzling" Point of Entry.

The classic Point of Entry includes a tour or a virtual tour, which may coincide with many of the program-oriented events that you already offer. For example, a school that always has a music performance on Wednesday mornings decided to have their Point of Entry Events on Wednesday mornings, so they could be sure to include a stop at the music performance on their tour. They had the music teacher talk about the correlation between participation in music class and math test scores and tell an inspiring story about a very shy girl who came out of her shell through her participation in the school choir, all while showing people through the music room, pointing out the piano that had been donated recently and the old donated drums that he was hoping to replace soon.

As an example of a Point of Entry in a Box, one Habitat for Humanity affiliate offered a one-hour Point of Entry during the lunch break at their weekly volunteer "build" day, walking people through each of the key steps of the Point of Entry. Volunteers knew in advance that, in addition to coming to build a house all day, there would be an optional one-hour program about the larger work of Habitat for Humanity in the community. There was a separate room off the lunch room for this session. People signed in with their contact information just for this special, inspiring Point of Entry "Habitour," and then went back to their volunteer work after lunch.

Here is the agenda for a Point of Entry. We will focus on the program elements first and then come back to look at possible venues, the best times to hold your Point of Entry Events, and which other events you might already have that would be suitable for converting into Point of Entry Events.

POINT OF ENTRY AGENDA

1. To start
   a. Greeting
   b. Sign in
   c. Mix and mingle
2. Program
   a. While seated
      - Welcome (board member)—3 minutes
      - Visionary Leader Talk—5 to 7 minutes
         ▲ Past, present, future
      - Questions and answers—3 minutes
   b. Walking around—30 to 40 minutes
      - Tour (real or virtual)
         ▲ Three stops
         ▲ Each stop: myth-buster fact, story, need
      - Live testimonial—3 to 5 minutes
3. Thank you and wrap up—2 minutes

TO START
Greeting

From the perspective of the guests, the Point of Entry Event begins as soon as they arrive and are greeted at the door or even at the curb.

Years ago, I designed a Point of Entry for a Christian school for African American students in Seattle where I developed the Benevon Model. For our rainy morning Point of Entry Events at a somewhat hard-to-find location, I would often stand out at the curb under an umbrella to greet people as they drove up. Be prepared to do whatever it takes to make your guests feel comfortable as they arrive.

Think about who will greet each of your visitors and where they will be stationed. Ideally, the greeter will be the person who invited them—friend, board member, etc. The next best choice is the development director or the person who will be their ongoing liaison with the organization. Note that you may want to save the executive director or CEO for a brief appearance later.

The greeter welcomes the guests, takes their coats, and walks with them to the sign-in table.

Sign-In: Capturing Names with Permission

The majority of your Point of Entry guests will have been invited to attend personally by a friend. They have been told that your organization is trying to spread the word in the community about its good work and that you are looking for feedback about how you are telling your story. They are told in advance that they will not be asked to give money at the Point of Entry.

Therefore, when they arrive that first day at the Point of Entry, they know that they are coming to a one-hour introductory event. They are coming to check out your work at the recommendation of a trusted friend. They are predisposed to like you. They are willing to give you their basic contact information.

The Sign-In Table

The sign-in table is the essential checkpoint through which all visitors must pass. A friendly, detail-oriented staff person or volunteer seated behind the table gives your visitors a sign-in card and waits while they fill it out. The only information you have enough permission to gather at this early stage is their name, address, phone number (whichever one they want to give you), e-mail address, and the name of the person who invited them to the Point of Entry Event. If guests ask what this is for, simply tell them that you would like to call them to follow up and get their feedback about the event.

Brief Mix-and-Mingle Time

As the rest of the guests are gathering, offer them a cup of coffee or tea, if appropriate, and introduce them to other visitors. This is a good time for the executive director or CEO to enter and be available for informal conversations. Point out pictures on the walls, displays, scrapbooks, or any special features of the room they are in.

PROGRAM (WHILE SEATED)

It is critical that everyone is seated during this portion of the Point of Entry because you want them to be focused on the program. Waiting for them at their seat is a packet of handouts that outline general information about your organization and your area of work.

Welcome (Three Minutes)

The program begins with a welcome greeting from a board member or volunteer who shares something personal about how they became involved with the organization. The guests need to know that this person really cares.

Visionary Leader Talk (Seven Minutes)

The Visionary Leader is the executive director or top-ranking paid staff member. If there are no paid staff members, the Visionary Leader is the person in the top volunteer role, usually the board chair.

The Visionary Leader speaks for five to seven minutes (no longer) about the past, present, and future of the organization, sharing their emotional connection to the work and a story about why they came to work here or what keeps them here.

We spend a great deal of time coaching Visionary Leaders to speak succinctly and passionately, getting to the heart of their love of the work, not droning on about facts, statistics, and programs with acronyms that will numb the guests. The talk must make it clear to the guests that the Visionary Leader sees clearly where the organization is going and that the organization needs support from the community in order to get there. In other words, the Visionary Leader must convey a clear sense of "the gap," as well as their plan, even if only loosely defined, for filling that gap. And they must do this with genuine emotion. The Visionary Leader Talk Worksheet is included in the Appendix.

Questions and Answers (Three Minutes)

At the end of this informational segment of the Point of Entry, the person who will be making the Follow-Up Calls to each guest asks for questions. This shows guests that the speaker is knowledgeable. Allow time for three or four questions. Invite those with more questions to stay after the meeting to talk further.

PROGRAM (WALKING AROUND)

During the next part of the program, guests get up and walk around. This portion of the program should last thirty to forty minutes.

Tour—Real or Virtual (Forty Minutes)

If you are able to take them on a real tour of your offices or facility, do that. If you are not able to walk them around because, for example, your work is highly confidential or you do not have anything to show them, you can do a stand-up-and-walk-around "virtual tour" right there in the same room where your sit-down portion of the Point of Entry was held, using displays in three of the corners or along the walls.

Three Stops

This tour—whether real or virtual—must include three stops (a fourth stop is optional). The three stops should be chosen based on their ability to showcase the breadth of your work. For example if you were to boil down everything that your group does into three "buckets," what might they be? For a group serving adults with disabilities, their three buckets might be: job training, housing, and transportation. Those three buckets would dictate the three tour stops.

Each Stop: Myth-Buster Fact, Story, Need

At each stop along the tour, you must give people a "myth-buster" fact, tell them a story about a life that was changed, and tell them an unmet need, all within that same program area.

For example, the aforementioned group might take people to the job training department where they see college students with severe physical disabilities taking a computer class. The instructor might come out to tell them that, contrary to people's expectations, 95% of their students are placed in businesses where they stay five years or longer. Then she might tell the story of Louise, a former student who arrived at the center two years ago, with no job skills, despondent after her mother had died. Thanks to the center's skilled and loving staff, they provided her with all the support she needed and specific job skills, and then arranged a great match at a company near her house. She has been there for over a year. In fact, she comes back to the center one night a week to help out in the computer training classroom and to inspire other students to keep going. The tour guide ends by describing an unmet need. "As proud as we are of Louise, we have over 100 students on our waiting list right now, sitting at home, hoping we will call to give them an opportunity to get to work."

Then the tour moves on to a stop about the housing program, where we again hear a myth-buster fact, a story, and a need. Sometimes the stories are told by staff, sometimes by the people themselves, sometimes by reading a letter from a former client or a family member. The stories need to be short and powerful.

We teach groups how to craft an Essential Story—that one representative story that showcases their organization's work—so that they learn how to go deep enough and still keep it short. What follows is an explanation of the stages of an Essential Story and a fill-in-the-blanks Essential Story template, which you can use for crafting your organization's Essential Story.

THREE STAGES OF AN ESSENTIAL STORY

ELEMENTS	SUGGESTED PHRASING
Stage 1: Before	
• Choose one person's story. • Briefly describe their situation before working with your organization. • What was their life like then? How difficult was it?	I'll never forget the story about Tom. Just a few years ago, Tom had a family and a job. Through a set of hard circumstances, he found himself hopeless and living under a bridge. He had fallen about as low as you can in our society. When I tell this story, it always reminds me of how much I take for granted in my own life, like a roof over my head, a hot shower every day, or even a hot meal. It is hard to imagine how he survived day-to-day.
Stage 2: Intervention	
• What brought this person into contact with your organization? • What services and support did they receive from you? • What was your personal observation of them at that time?	Someone mentioned to Tom that he could get a decent meal at our shelter. I will never forget the look in his eyes the first time he visited us. He was so embarrassed to have to take what he called a "handout." Every day Tom came to the shelter, he gained strength. He started to talk to others at the dinner table. We helped him learn computer skills so he was able to get a job in a new field. We provided hope for him. We helped him regain a sense of pride and self esteem. He was so proud of what he was accomplishing. I saw him in class one day tutoring one of the other new students who was struggling to learn to use the computer keyboard.

continued on next page

continued from previous page

THREE STAGES OF AN ESSENTIAL STORY

ELEMENTS	SUGGESTED PHRASING
Stage 3: After	
• What are the results of the intervention? How has life changed for this person? • What is now possible for them? • What does this person now say about their life? • How are they "giving back" to others?	Getting involved with our organization gave Tom a new future for his life. Tom is thriving now. He has an apartment, a job, and seems to be on top of the world. He volunteers with us when he has the time. He walked up to me a month or so ago, gave me a big hug, and told me that our organization had literally saved his life. He drives by that bridge every now and then and it reminds him how lucky he is. He says he won't quit until everyone under that bridge gets the same chance he did. This is what people tell us all the time: "You people know no limits to caring."

ESSENTIAL STORY TEMPLATE

I'll never forget the story about _____.

1. Before _____ (name) found (came to, got involved with) _____ (our organization), her life was _____. So many of the things that you and I take for granted, such as _____ _____, just weren't possible for _____ (name). It seemed to _____ that this would never change.

2. _____ found (came to, was referred to) _____ (our organization) by _____. Within _____ months (years), _____'s life turned around. Rather than _____ _____, she was _____. Our _____ (specific, jargon-free) programs taught _____ to _____ and helped her get back on her feet again. People who saw _____ back then said she was _____ (a changed person, full of life again, able to look you in the eye). Really, what we provided her was _____ ____ (a sense of pride, dignity, confidence, strength, courage) to get back out there and be a good _____ (parent, student).

3. Now, _____ is thriving. She has (is, does) _____. She says life will never be the same. Every time she thinks about (goes back to) _____, she says she thanks _____ for (giving her back her pride, her children, saving her life, her education, her dignity). The last time I saw her she was _____ (or: she came back to see us recently and said _____).

_____ is just one example of the lives that are being changed every day here at _____.

Live Testimonial (Three to Five Minutes)

End your real or virtual tour with a live testimonial from someone whose life has been changed (like Louise) at the door as people are ready to walk out. People will never forget this.

THANK YOU AND WRAP UP

Have your board member or volunteer who opened the program be the person to wrap it up. Thank guests for taking their time to come.

Let them know you would like to call them in the next week to get their feedback and advice. This wrap-up portion should last just two minutes. Do not sit back down and do a wrap-up session with the whole group at the end. It is far better to debrief with them one-on-one by phone in the next few days after they have digested what they saw. Of course, if people want to linger at the door with a few more questions or comments, that is fine.

OTHER FACTORS TO CONSIDER
Selecting Your "Cast"

For a full-scale Point of Entry, your cast will include the host (a board member or volunteer), the Visionary Leader, and the development director or designated fundraising person who will be making the Follow-Up Calls. You will want to make sure that the follow-up person is prominently placed in the program so people will remember him or her. In addition, the live Testimonial Speaker will need to be part of your "cast." Over time, you may find ways to streamline the number of people needed to produce your Point of Entry. For example, the board member might also be the Testimonial Speaker at the end if they have a personal story to share.

Let's look at the individual components that make up a successful and memorable Point of Entry, all while making it sustainable for you and your team to produce on an ongoing basis.

The Venue

Most often, the Point of Entry will be an event—a gathering of real people in real time to learn about your program. The classic Point of Entry is a tour. If your organization lends itself at all to a tour, this should definitely be your preferred Point of Entry.

Even if you think there would not be much for people to see at your office, there is a lot you can do to spruce it up and turn it into the perfect venue for a Point of Entry. You can add photos to the walls and tell a story about what goes on in each room as you walk people through. Stopping by the desk of a hard-working staff person to have them share an anecdote about someone who has benefited from their program will make a big impact, as will having someone read a testimonial letter from a grateful former client in your conference room.

If you are concerned about the confidential nature of what people might see on a tour, there are ways to highlight only the programs or clients you want them to see. Many excellent Point of Entry Events have been done in one room only, without ever walking people through the facility. By using photos and live testimonials, you can paint a powerful picture that people will never forget. If your Point of Entry is on-site or in your office, people will feel more connected to your organization. They will remember you best if they have physically been to your site.

If you conclude that you cannot have an on-site tour, here are some other examples of venues for your Point of Entry:

- A box-lunch at a board member's office.
- Evening "house parties" in people's homes.
- A one-on-one meeting anywhere.
- An alumni gathering in each of your regions or cities.

Ideal Size

The ideal size for a regularly scheduled, on-site Point of Entry is somewhere between ten and fifteen people. This allows for personal interaction and a manageable follow-up schedule.

Having said that, there are many exceptions. One large university medical research institution puts on a major high-end Point of Entry Event once a year. Tightly choreographed and held on a Saturday morning, this event educates and inspires 150 guests. All guests attend the president's Visionary Leader Talk before being divided into smaller groups (pre-selected by the guests) where medical researchers each present the Facts 101 and the Emotional Hook about their respective research. The morning concludes with a lovely lunch back in the larger group, allowing for the sharing of ideas among guests. Guests are guided through the process by the staff member who will be their ongoing liaison to the organization.

At the other extreme, your Point of Entry does not need to be done in a group at all. You could do a One-on-One Point of Entry with a person sitting next to you on an airplane or standing next to you in a long line. It doesn't have to take a long time. We will talk more about the One-on-One Point of Entry in the next chapter.

High Touch/Low Tech
You will notice there is no video or PowerPoint used at a Point of Entry. It is intentionally designed to be more informal, high-touch, and person-to-person, as if a group of close friends are sitting around a table talking about something they all care about. Do not be tempted to deviate from this format if you want your Point of Entry to sizzle.

Handouts at Your Point of Entry Event
What follows is an outline of the handouts for your guests at your Point of Entry Events.
1. Fact Sheet
   - Three FAQs
   - Graphic (i.e., pie chart, bar graph)
2. Wish List
   - Small to large
   - Ten items maximum
   - Things you really want
   - Volunteer positions
   - No prices or monetary amounts
3. Brochure—basic version (optional)
4. Dates of future Point of Entry Events
5. Other optional materials
   - Photos
   - Brag book

Timing
Your full Point of Entry should last one hour—no longer.
   Deciding when to have your Point of Entry Events takes experimentation and depends on where they will be held. Your first consideration should be the time that is most convenient for your guests. If you are asking them to come to an out-of-the-way location, what time

of day is easiest for them to get there? Working people might prefer early morning, late in the day, or lunchtime. Stay-at-home parents and retired people may prefer midday.

Next, consider the best time to show them your programs or take them on your tour. If you are planning to include live testimonials from staff or program participants, what times of day are those programs in session? Even within the work day, there may be certain times when there is more to see than others. For example, times when the kids are the freshest or the volunteers are the busiest. Many arts organizations will hold their Point of Entry Events in conjunction with a rehearsal or preview showing, which dictates the best dates and times. This is often the case with Free Feel-Good Cultivation Events (also called Point of Re-Entry Events), such as alumni weekend reunions or other recognition events, which we will discuss further in Chapter 8.

Do not overlook evenings and weekends as good times to hold your Point of Entry Events. Those times work best for many people. For example, a faith-based retirement home holds its Point of Entry on Sundays at lunchtime, which is when family members usually come to visit their elderly parents and grandparents. As mentioned before, many Habitat for Humanity affiliates put on their Point of Entry on Saturdays at lunch, in conjunction with their home building. That is the time when their morning volunteers and afternoon volunteers overlap and take a break. Weeknights in people's living rooms often work well for grass-roots and women's organizations.

Finally, after testing various times, many groups decide to offer their regularly scheduled Point of Entry Events at two alternating times each month—for example, one in the morning and one in the early afternoon—to make them convenient and accessible for everyone.

Naming Your Point of Entry

Take the time to choose a clever, inviting name for your Point of Entry. The term "Point of Entry" is for your internal use only. It is much too clinical to use with the general public.

One Benevon workshop participant team from an organ-donor program named their Point of Entry Events "Lifesaver Events." One Red Cross chapter named theirs "The Red Cross Experience." One organization that serves abused children calls their Point of Entry "If These Walls Could Talk." A Girl Scout council calls theirs "Beyond the Cookie Box." Other groups call theirs names such as "Meet Family Services," "Getting to Know Your Humane Society," "Village Theater 101," or even something as generic as "Tuesday Tours." Find something unique and clever that reflects your mission in some way.

Frequency

You should be putting on Point of Entry Events one or two times per month. Therefore, choose a venue and time of day that can work on a repetitive basis, such as the first Thursday morning and the third Thursday afternoon of each month.

Sustainability of the Point of Entry

We tell the groups in our Sustainable Funding Program that once they adopt the Benevon Model, they should assume they will be putting on Point of Entry Events for the rest of their organization's life! That becomes a powerful wake-up call to everyone to be sure that each element is sustainable. Having to muster up new tour guides, speakers, and stops on the tour each month is a recipe for failure. It may take you up to twelve Point of Entry Events to experiment with the best format, time of day, venue, etc. But once you get it right (as measured by only one statistic: at least 25% of your Point of Entry guests refer others to attend subsequent Point of Entry Events), don't change a thing.

CONVERTING EXISTING PROGRAM EVENTS INTO POINT OF ENTRY EVENTS

As you have been reading this description of the classic Benevon Point of Entry, perhaps you have been thinking of other events your organization is already putting on that could be modified to become Point of Entry Events. Note that the only real candidates for conversion to Point of Entry Events are the regularly scheduled volunteer-recruitment events or other events that are informational in nature and open to the public. We will discuss several examples of these events below.

A few cautions: Do not try to convert a one-time event like the students' annual music performance into a Point of Entry. Odds are those should be saved for Free Feel-Good Cultivation Events. Do not convert any existing fundraising event into a Point of Entry—those are to be saved for what we call Point of Entry Conversion Events.

Even if you do not have any of these regularly scheduled informational events, you may have other repeating programs that could provide the emotional elements and scheduled tour stops during your Point of Entry Events. For example:

- A faith-based school: Wednesday morning chapel led by the students.
- An arts academy: Tuesday morning music assembly.
- A theater group: a backstage tour and talk with the artistic director just before a rehearsal.
- A school for children with special needs: a science night where the kids proudly show off their experiments.
- A food bank: Thursday afternoons when the volunteers are packing the backpacks to give school kids to take home with food for their families for the weekend.

In each of these cases, you would still need to follow the Point of Entry agenda, inserting one of these program occasions as a stop along the tour. Just be sure that as you "show off" this program or project, you tell your guests at least one fact about this program or the participants in it, a story about someone whose life was changed thanks to this program, and an unmet need related to the program. Do not assume that your guests will be able to draw these conclusions on their own.

Here are some more examples of regularly scheduled events that could be converted to classic Point of Entry Events.

Converting an Open House

Some nonprofits have regularly scheduled open houses or tours that are open to the community and advertised in their local newspapers. These convert nicely into Point of Entry Events, if the following modifications are made.

First, you must change the name of the event. "Open house" implies drop in, mingle, and leave whenever you like. A Point of Entry is not that casual. It has a set start and end time and a formal program in between. Be sure to clearly tell people that the format of the event is changing. Or, better yet, tell them you will no longer be offering open houses, and instead, you will be offering a firsthand tour of your organization that will last no longer than one hour. Give them the exact start and end time and tell them they must RSVP.

Second, while you may continue the announcements in the newspaper as one means of inviting people to your monthly Point of Entry Events, this is not the preferred way to invite people. The classic Point of Entry works best when people are invited word-of-mouth by a friend—someone who has already been inspired at a similar Point of Entry. The sooner you can get the word-of-mouth "snowball" effect working in your favor, the sooner the Benevon Model will become sustainable within your organization.

Once you have made these two modifications, you can design a great event following the Point of Entry agenda, including the Visionary Leader Talk, the tour stops, the live testimonial, etc.

Converting a Volunteer-Recruitment Event

Many groups that are heavily dependent on volunteers have regularly scheduled recruitment events. They use these as an opportunity to tell people about their programs in general and their volunteer programs in particular. Not everyone who attends ends up wanting to volunteer for the particular positions needed. Often, those people who choose not to volunteer leave without getting involved at all.

By converting the volunteer-recruitment event into a Point of Entry, people leave with a broader sense of the mission and, in the Follow-Up Call after the Point of Entry, they may choose to become involved in other ways.

The easiest way to convert a volunteer-recruitment event is to append a thirty-minute volunteer-recruitment meeting onto a classic one-hour Point of Entry. In other words, when you invite people, tell them that the first hour will be an introductory session about the mission and work of the organization and the next thirty minutes will be a more specific presentation of the various volunteer opportunities available.

This format works well in both respects. You can use the first hour as your standard monthly Point of Entry. Some people may surprise you and choose to stay the extra thirty minutes to find out about volunteer opportunities. Just be sure they are told in the invitation process that there is no obligation for them to do so. Conversely, people coming to learn about volunteering may be exposed to other aspects of your program that interest them, and they may have friends who they would like to refer. Plus, as stated above, they may not choose to volunteer after all, yet they could still spread the word about your group and ultimately become donors.

A final thought about this conversion example: we often work with groups that do not have any traditional volunteer opportunities due to the confidential nature of their work, location, etc. Once they start putting on monthly Point of Entry Events, in the subsequent Follow-Up Call, when they ask people, "Is there any way you could see yourself getting involved here?" people often ask how they can volunteer. We have coached these groups to tell people that they need help spreading the word about their organization at similar Point of Entry Events, and they ask these people to volunteer in their fundraising program by hosting Point of Entry Events or helping to put them on. In fact, some people are shy about hands-on volunteering with your clients and may prefer this more administrative role.

Converting a Featured Speaker Series

Does your group have a monthly speaker's series going on? These speakers are usually speaking on topics relevant to the organization's mission, so they make great opportunities for attaching onto a classic Point of Entry. Especially for newcomers who may be coming to hear the speaker without really knowing much about your organization, the Point of Entry can be a refreshing addition, so long as you warn people in advance that it is available and don't just surprise them with it.

In this case, you can offer a little food and give it more of a reception feel, although it still has a definite start and end time and follows the classic agenda. I have seen this work well in hospitals and churches where they have a great speaker series lined up. Without offering this optional Point of Entry before the speaker starts, many guests would leave inspired by the speaker and never make the connection to your mission. That is the job of the organization to do.

Another nice touch is to have the speaker say a few (pre-scripted) words about how the work of your organization relates to his or her topic. Of course, someone from your staff can make some remarks at the start of the program, thanking people for coming and asking anyone who would like to be invited back for one of your "informational tours, like the one we had earlier this evening," to fill out a card, turn in a business card, etc.

Converting a Theater Rehearsal

This falls more accurately into the category of a "tour stop" than a full Point of Entry opportunity, but I include it here because it is often overlooked as the rich, mission-focused, sizzling moment that potential theater goers crave. Getting to sit in on all or part of a rehearsal is thrilling. If you precede it with a Point of Entry backstage tour with a brief Visionary Leader Talk from the artistic director and a testimonial or two from a stagehand or actor, you will have everyone completely inspired. Then having them stay for a slice of the show pulls it all together. You can bet those people will be referring others when you call them to follow up.

Converting an Art Opening Night
Visual arts shows present a similar opportunity. Opening nights or tours with the curator through new shows are very attractive opportunities to combine with a classic Point of Entry. The art is the Emotional Hook for people, and the passion of the curator and the beautiful show will be enough to make art lovers call their friends. Combined with a visit to a sketch class out in the garden and a tour stop in the storage area of archived art, you will have truly inspired your guests. Also, that tour of the storage area is a great place to talk about the need for more space, more technologically up-to-date storage facilities, etc.

Converting a Red Cross CPR Saturday
Several years ago, when the American Red Cross had a major program going to educate everyone in CPR, they would take over huge gymnasiums and have marathon CPR classes. They offered people the opportunity to come thirty minutes early to learn more about the work of the Red Cross. Off to the side of the gymnasium, they had two tented booths with chairs for people to come in, fill out a card with their contact information, sit down, and attend a Point of Entry before they went to their CPR class. It worked beautifully. As you might imagine, the testimonials were stories from people who had either saved a life or been saved by someone who had—fortunately—been trained in CPR by the American Red Cross.

Converting a Habitat for Humanity House Dedication
These are some of the most emotional events you can find. That wonderful day when the hard-working, well-deserving (often single-parent) family receives the keys to their new house and a Bible. On the lawn out in front of the home, the recipient family gets to say a few words of thanks (while everyone else is wiping away the tears). Appending a Point of Entry onto the beginning of this event really anchors the work of Habitat for Humanity in reality. Otherwise, it would be easy for people to presume that the family was given that house as a charitable gift, rather than knowing how many hours of sweat equity they had to put into it and what they will need to do to retain and maintain it.

Again, just be sure to invite people word-of-mouth and to tell them in advance that this is a separate special meeting prior to the house dedication to give them more information about Habitat for Humanity. In other words, they need to know it is not a fundraising event—they will not be asked for money.

Converting a Holiday Event

Holiday events make wonderful opportunities for Point of Entry Events. In fact, I often wish people would take the time to treat the holiday season for what it could be—one big Point of Entry opportunity. See Chapter 13 for more ideas about how to missionize all of your holiday events.

Now let's move on to some Point of Entry variations.

CHAPTER 6

POINT OF ENTRY VARIATIONS

Now that you understand the basics of the classic Point of Entry, we can look at three common variations.

THE POINT OF ENTRY IN A BOX

Once you have refined your Point of Entry and are getting that 25% referral rate regularly, the event will have become routine for you. At our school in Seattle, I remember getting to a point when we were conducting our morning tours up to three times a week! I could arrive at the school, take out my "Point of Entry box," complete with name tags, sign-in cards, and handouts, and set up the event in under half an hour.

That's when we realized our Point of Entry had become generic and repeatable enough that we could take it to a board member's conference room, a volunteer's living room, or a church hall and put on a Point of Entry in a Box. You still need to bring at least one other speaker along, ideally a Testimonial Speaker, to keep the presentation lively and compelling. This ability to vary the venue will allow you to ramp up your guest numbers substantially, as long as the guests know that they are coming to a Point of Entry about your organization.

Examples of Point of Entry Events in a Box
Corporate Lunch Hours
The perfect way to engage your corporate sponsors "where they live" is to take your Point of Entry to their corporate offices or lunchrooms for (optional) lunch-time presentations for their employees. Nonprofits

are often so grateful for a corporate gift that they neglect to ask for the real prize: the right to tell their story to the employees directly. A simple, heartfelt Point of Entry in a Box will win over many employees (whose subsequent gifts might qualify for corporate matching dollars as well). Arrange this through your main contact at the corporation, and make sure your program includes your Visionary Leader and a live Testimonial Speaker (and no video). Be sure you are involved in preparing the invitation wording to the employees so that they know their attendance is truly optional and that if they attend, you will be calling them after the event to get their feedback. These can be recurring events with the same corporation, especially if they are "sizzling."

Dessert or Wine and Cheese Parties

We often hear from groups that their office or center is not conveniently located or that volunteers and board members who love their work have offered to host gatherings in their homes. These work well as Point of Entry Events in a Box, as long as the guests are told in advance what they are being invited to, the program lasts one hour or less, and there is no "soft" Ask during the event. These events run the risk of having people make a donation right on the spot, as a courtesy to the host or hostess. It is not easy to shift that mindset. Again, be sure you write or approve the invitation wording so guests know in advance what they are coming to—an introductory session about your work. Also, be sure there is not a full dinner served. Dessert or wine and cheese are fine.

As far as timing, it is fine to hold the event from 5:00 p.m.–7:00 p.m., for example, or from 8:00 p.m.–9:00 p.m. for a dessert gathering, as long as you let people know in the invitation that there will be a program that starts and ends at a set time. Have sign-in cards and a greeter at the door. The program should include your Visionary Leader and many of the same story elements from your classic Point of Entry, with the addition of a testimonial from the host or hostess if they have had a firsthand experience with your work. Be sure to make your Follow-Up Calls, and when people ask how they can get involved, suggest that they host a similar event in their home or office. This is a great strategy for grass-roots groups that may not have a formal office at all, and also for groups that are just getting started and want to get the word out in the community.

A Board Member's Office

You can see how easily the Point of Entry format can be adapted to an office conference room or country club private dining room setting. The biggest risk here is the subtle—and sometimes, not-so-subtle—pressure that the guests may feel to give money on the spot. Well-meaning, old-school hosts often gently nudge their friends to attend and to be prepared to give. If you sense that possibility with your host, it may be best to politely decline the offer, encouraging the host to invite these same friends to your primary Point of Entry at your office, where you will have more control over the program agenda. Having said that, if the host understands that the purpose of a Point of Entry is merely to introduce people to the organization, and they are still willing to put together a private lunch or meeting, by all means, go for it! Again, don't skip any of the steps: sign-in cards, powerful program, and Follow-Up Calls.

THE ONE-ON-ONE POINT OF ENTRY

Once you see the power of the Point of Entry, you can see the potential for Point of Entry "moments" everywhere—sitting next to a stranger on a train or airplane, in a line at the grocery store, or standing at the punchbowl at a holiday party.

While the core of your Point of Entry program will most likely always be your classic Point of Entry Events in your office or main location, there will be many occasions when your board members, volunteers, and staff will find themselves naturally in a position to have a brief conversation with a friend or colleague about your organization. This is especially useful for busy executive directors and board members who are already interacting with high-level people in your community on other matters. By inserting a brief Point of Entry element into the course of their conversation, these same friends and colleagues will be connected to your work, and they may give you permission to stay in contact with them.

Whether or not they choose to learn more, you will have spread the word, and perhaps in a Follow-Up Call they will elect to come to a "real" Point of Entry Event or to refer someone else who truly is passionate about your mission.

In the coaching that follows our workshops, we often hear remarkable stories from people who do these One-on-One Point of Entry "moments" with old friends or strangers. Once you refine the elements and give them to your board members or other insiders, with a little practice, they will feel prepared to educate and genuinely move someone to tears about the great work of your organization in less than three minutes!

Here are the points that must be covered in the One-on-One Point of Entry. Although this looks like a stilted agenda, it will flow very naturally in a give-and-take dialog.

Elements of the One-on-One Point of Entry

1. **Who we are.** You have to tell them the name of your organization.
2. **Our top three program areas.** Even if you have fifteen or twenty programs, figure out which three "buckets" you will put them all in. You can use the same three program areas that you showcase in your live Point of Entry.
3. **One little-known fact about our work.** Here is where you insert a myth-buster fact from your standard Point of Entry. These are the facts that dispel people's unspoken stereotypes and myths about your work. Make it interesting and easy to remember.
4. **Why I work here.** Here is where you tell your own story—the short version. Let them know this is much more than a job for you. If you lost a family member to the disease you are now working to cure, tell them that. People respect a personal connection. If you don't have such a connection that drew you to the organization, tell them what keeps you working there.

5. **"I'll never forget the story about..."** This is where you tell the Essential Story—again, the short version. Practice telling it until you can do it in thirty seconds or less. It can be done.
6. **"Would you be interested in more information?"** or "Would you like to come to our regularly scheduled tour?" If they are interested, ask for their business card and give them yours.

That's it. In less than three minutes, you have conveyed the Facts 101 and the Emotional Hook. Then be quiet and listen closely to the person's response. Even if they are not personally interested in the work of your organization, if you have moved them with the facts and the stories, they will have been touched enough to thank you and suggest other people they know who you might want to contact. At best, they will jump right in and offer to help you or say that they want to learn more by coming to one of your regularly scheduled Point of Entry Events.

When you get back to your office, be sure this person's name gets added to your database and to your follow-up tracking system. If they said they would like to come to a Point of Entry Event, you need to be the one to call and personally invite them. Do not delegate this to anyone else. Remember, this personal connection is key to the success of the Benevon Model. Make it as easy as possible for them to say yes. You can even encourage them to bring a friend, if that would make them feel more comfortable.

If you train your board and volunteers to do One-on-One Point of Entry Events, they will become your roving ambassadors in the community. Whenever they attend social events or business gatherings, they will be armed and ready to go.

THE PRE-POINT OF ENTRY EVENT

There is one last type of event that is not officially a part of our model at all, but I include them here because they happen all the time, are a great source of visibility for nonprofits, and are often confused with a Point of Entry in a Box. These are events hosted by other groups—like

Rotary Club meetings, church mission nights, United Way agency presentations, etc.—where you are invited to come and tell people about your organization. Do not confuse these events with a Point of Entry in a Box.

At a Point of Entry in a Box, your organization is in the driver's seat. You choose the time and location, and you can manage the process of inviting the guests to be sure that they have been invited word-of-mouth by someone who is passionate about your work. You can ensure that guests were told in advance that they are invited to a one-hour session to learn about the work of the organization and that they will be asked for their feedback after the event, but they will not be asked for money at this event.

In other words, at a Point of Entry in a Box, you can control the key elements of the Point of Entry and gain direct permission from the guests to make Follow-Up Calls to each of them.

Conversely, when your organization is invited to speak at another group's meeting, you do not have that control or permission. Even if the purpose of the group you are speaking to appears to be completely consistent with your mission, do not presume that you have permission to ask people individually for their contact information or to follow up with them.

We work with a Lutheran social services organization that operates a downtown shelter and food bank in a notoriously high-crime area. A large Lutheran church invited the group to come to their Thursday night meeting of the church missions committee to give a thirty-minute presentation about the shelter's work. The executive director of the shelter gave a compelling talk about the spiritual nature of their work and what keeps her there every day, including many stories about how the organization is changing lives every day. Then a former client told her story. People were moved to tears.

But because she was a guest speaker at the church's meeting, the executive director and her staff wisely knew in advance that they would not have the explicit permission to make Follow-Up Calls to each attendee.

Anticipating this situation, she converted the speaking opportunity into a Pre-Point of Entry, by ending the thirty-minute presentation with an invitation for anyone interested in knowing more about the work of the shelter, getting more involved, or coming out to take one of their "Mission Tours," to please see her after the meeting to give her their business cards or contact information.

Although not everyone gave her their contact information at the end of the meeting, she knew that the people who did seek her out were truly interested in learning more and would be looking forward to her Follow-Up Call.

Her next step was to invite them to a Point of Entry and then take them around the cycle, obtaining their permission before each subsequent step.

Can you see the application of this to civic group presentations or other special meetings where you are invited to be a guest presenter? These are wonderful opportunities to tell your organization's story in the community. They build interest and goodwill. Accept these invitations graciously, and make your presentation as compelling and emotional as you would make at a true Point of Entry.

Just know that, unlike your own Point of Entry that you host at your office or program site, these Pre-Point of Entry Events allow you to do the one-on-one follow-up *only* with the people who seek you out at the end and ask for more information. If your presentation is riveting, there should be many of them anxious to speak with you!

You can see that there are many subtleties as you get into customizing the model. Just stay true to your own instincts, and do not override the limited amount of permission you may have from a guest to follow up with them. That is why, in the long run, the classic Point of Entry is by far the cleanest, most transparent, and most productive way to connect with people who really care about your work. Treat them the way you would want to be treated. You cannot make Follow-Up Calls to every person who attended a Rotary meeting where you spoke. You only have enough permission to call those who came up to you at the end of the meeting and gave you their business card so you could give them additional information.

A WORD OF CAUTION

Before we move on to the next type of event—the Free One-Hour Ask Event—let me leave you with one final caution about Point of Entry Events. All this talk of converting existing events into Point of Entry Events might make it sound like a full calendar of random events would suffice for an ongoing Point of Entry system. Not so. Even if you do have many other opportunities for converting events to Point of Entry Events, you must still host classic monthly Point of Entry Events at your main office, center, or site if you intend to use this model long-term. There is no substitute for that.

CHAPTER 7

THE FREE ONE-HOUR ASK EVENT

Now, let's move on to the second type of event in our model, the Benevon Free One-Hour Ask Event. In this chapter, I will describe the event in more detail and discuss options for converting other events you may already be putting on into an Ask Event.

Please do not attempt to put on this event unless you have already been doing the first two steps of the model. As tempting as it may be to rush to the Ask Event by skipping over the Point of Entry and follow-up process, you will be doing a significant disservice to your organization in the long run.

We receive so many calls from disappointed development directors who try the Ask Event in desperation to raise fast money, only to find that it has backfired in many predictable ways. Please be forewarned: the Ask Event is the third step (not the first step!) in the Benevon Model. It is the culmination or harvesting of a long planting, tending, and cultivating process. Rushing ahead to the Ask Event causes many more problems for your organization than it solves.

To further distinguish the Ask Event from other events you may know of, let's look at the key requirements for the event to qualify as a Benevon Ask Event.

Guests must be invited word-of-mouth by a friend (not by printed invitations) to sit at their table of ten people. When guests are invited, they are told that this one-hour event is free to attend and that it is a fundraising event, but there is no requirement to give at all (no minimum, no maximum). As much as anything, you want guests to come to learn about the wonderful work of your organization.

At least 40% (20% in year one) of the Ask Event guests must have attended a prior Point of Entry Event and received a Follow-Up Call and one or two subsequent personal contacts. In other words, a

40% critical mass of people at the event are now well aware of your work and ready to make a financial commitment. They are looking forward to attending the event and bringing their friends to learn more as well.

The event is a well-rehearsed, tightly choreographed mix of compelling facts, stories, music, video, and testimonials, culminating in a "pitch" when people are invited to join a Multiple-Year Giving Society, making a pledge to give your organization at least $1,000 a year for each of the next five years. Here is a template of a pledge card.

PLEDGE CARD / FREE ONE-HOUR ASK EVENT

Organization Name
Name of Event
Fundraising (Breakfast/Lunch)

I would like to become a founding member of the (Multiple-Year Giving Society):
___ (First Unit of Service): $1,000 per year for 5 years
___ (Second Unit of Service): $10,000 per year for 5 years
___ (Third Unit of Service): $25,000 per year for 5 years

I would like to contribute in other ways:
___ Contribute $_____ for ___ years.
___ Please contact me. I have other thoughts to share.

Payment:
___ My check is enclosed, made payable to:
___ Please charge my Visa/MC # _____ Exp. _____
___ Please contact me about paying my pledge with stock.
___ My company will match my gift.

We will bill you in (month) for your annual pledge, unless you request otherwise.

Signature: _____

Date _____
Name _____
Organization _____
Address _____
City _____ State _____ Zip _____
Day Phone (___) _____ Evening Phone (___) _____
E-mail Address _____

There are three giving levels in the Multiple-Year Giving Society, which you name and never change. There are two options for these levels, depending on past giving history in your organization. The first option is to have levels of $1,000, $5,000, and $10,000 a year for the next five years. The second option is to have levels of $1,000, $10,000, and $25,000 a year for the next five years.

Groups we train and coach in our Curriculum for Sustainable Funding raise an average of over $200,000 in gifts and pledges in the first year. Only 40%–50% of the guests give any amount at the Ask Event, including the "fill-in-the-blanks" box. Approximately 10%–15% of the guests join the Multiple-Year Giving Society at one of the top three giving levels. We do not have statistics on the results of groups who implement the model on their own, but I would recommend that you reduce these predictions substantially if you are planning to try this without our training and coaching.

To determine the benchmark for a successful Ask Event, take the number of people who attend the Ask Event and divide that number by two. Then multiply the remaining number by $1,000 to determine how much money your event should raise. In other words, an event with 200 people in attendance should raise at least $100,000 in gifts and pledges.

All of the funds raised at the Ask Event, even after you have been having this Ask Event for many years, must be used for the unrestricted operating needs of the organization. For those major donors who may also wish to give to your capital or endowment programs, their gift at the Ask Event becomes their basic unrestricted gift each year.

The payoff rate on the pledges should be over 95%. That is because you do not merely invoice donors for each of the next five years and then wait to invite them back to the Ask Event in the sixth year! Rather, you begin the deeper cultivation process on the day after the first Ask Event they attend. Their multiple-year pledge at one of your higher giving levels needs to be regarded as the donor's way of telling you that they truly believe in your work and want to stay connected to you, perhaps learning more and becoming even more involved.

There is a place on the pledge card at the Ask Event where donors may make a gift of any amount for any number of years. It is the "fill-in-the-blanks" box. Most donors who use this box give up to $1,000 a year for one or two years only. As generous a gift as that is, it represents a different level of commitment than a larger, five-year pledge.

You must follow up the day after the Ask Event with a personal telephone call to thank each donor. Using the Benevon Five-Step Follow-Up Call, ask the donors for their feedback on the event, if they would like to become more involved, and if there is anyone else they would like to introduce to the organization. At this point, most of your happy new Multiple-Year Giving Society Donors will tell you how impressed they were by the Ask Event and that they wished they had invited more people!

That is when you close the loop of the Benevon Model—by inviting them to become Table Captains at next year's Ask Event, and, between now and this time next year, to introduce their friends to your organization by inviting them to a Point of Entry. In the coming year, if they send or bring their friends to a Point of Entry, you will educate and inspire them, follow up, and "bless and release" them if they are not interested or cultivate and involve them if they wish to know more. By the time they are sitting at your donor's table next year at the Ask Event, these guests will have been well-cultivated and ready to give.

After the first Ask Event, your job shifts dramatically to focusing on tending and further cultivating these new Multiple-Year Giving Society Donors. You do that by inviting them to Free Feel-Good Cultivation Events, also called Point of Re-Entry Events, which we will discuss in the next chapter.

THE ASK EVENT PROGRAM

Here is an overview of the Benevon Ask Event program. If you are seriously considering putting on an Ask Event, you should read my prior book, *Raising More Money—The Ask Event Handbook*, which goes into far greater detail on every aspect of this event. My purpose in the description that follows is to give you enough information to decide whether or not you want to add this event to your repertoire or, if you have chosen to adopt the entire Benevon Model, to do away with one of your other fundraising events and replace it with an Ask Event.

Day of Event
There is an air of excitement and anticipation! People are greeted at the front door of the hotel or other building by someone who is involved with your program—a student, a volunteer, a recipient of your services, or a family member. With music playing in the background, people pick up their nametags in the lobby area and are shown to their tables, where they are greeted warmly by their friend the Table Captain who invited them personally to attend.

Program Elements
Welcome and Thank You (Three Minutes)
The event begins at exactly the designated start time with a welcome and thank you from the board chair or emcee—someone who has a direct connection to the organization. Even if you are fortunate enough to have a professional media person agree to emcee your event, make sure that they have a personal reason for caring about the work of your organization.

Do not expect everyone to be in their seats on time waiting for the event to begin. There will still be many empty seats. Tempted as you may be to delay due to low attendance at the start time, do not start late. It will throw off the timing of the entire event. The script for the welcome includes thanking the board members, Table Captains, and any special guests. This takes about three minutes, during which time many more guests will arrive.

Opening Emotional Hook (Three Minutes)
While the term "Emotional Hook" may sound crass, this element is essential to the program. It is designed to connect people emotionally to your mission within the first five minutes of the event. You want your guests to know right away that you have something meaningful

and important to tell them about; you did not invite them here just to have breakfast. This opening Emotional Hook could be a child reading a poem, a candle-lighting ceremony, someone singing a song related to the mission, or an inspiring invocation. One domestic violence group played a recording of a 911 emergency call, and another group showed the video of their new thirty-second public service announcement. The opening Emotional Hook sets the tone for the entire event. It wakes people up to your mission and piques their interest for more.

Eat and Socialize (Ten Minutes)

This is the only "down time" in the one-hour program. People need a few minutes to socialize and connect with people at their table. The emcee has told them the program will start back up in ten minutes and encouraged them to look at their table tents (folded-over pieces of paper) in front of each person's place, displaying something that personalizes the work of the organization and educates people about the mission. For example, one American Lung Association event had photos of kids at asthma camp with stories by each child about why they look forward all year long to going to asthma camp. Other groups have cards with statistics about the disease that they are working to cure or the percentages of various toxic chemicals contained in certain foods. People are encouraged to pass these cards around so others can learn from them as well.

This social time is also the part of the program when the guests may receive a small take-away item, delivered personally to their tables by a volunteer, program participant, or family member. The purpose is not to give people a valuable object, but rather to connect them to the work of the organization even during this down time. Think about what you could give people that would tie into your program and your mission and how it could be delivered or presented to them personally as they sit at their tables.

For example, the same event that had the stories about asthma camp had camp-aged kids passing around plastic straws in little cellophane bags with bows. Later in the program, the guests were asked to squeeze the straws until they were partially closed and then inhale through them, to experience what it feels like to have an asthma attack.

One group serving homebound elderly individuals passed out holiday greeting cards and pens and asked the event guests to write a card to one of the people they serve. Other gifts may be less experiential, like apples, pens, bookmarks, pins, or buttons, yet they are delivered to each guest personally by someone involved with the organization.

Visionary Leader Talk (Five Minutes)
Now it is time for the leader of the organization to share the vision for the future. The Visionary Leader Talk is the anchor element of your Ask Event. It is worth taking the time to craft it carefully and rehearse it several times, coaching your Visionary Leader to deliver the talk powerfully, following the script.

Every organization has a Visionary Leader. This is usually the executive director or top-ranking paid staff member. If the organization does not have paid staff, the board chair generally serves as the Visionary Leader. While you may think your Visionary Leader does not always sound visionary or, conversely, may sound too visionary for most people, there is a way to craft a Visionary Leader Talk for every organization.

The Visionary Leader Talk at the Ask Event is similar to the Visionary Leader Talk at the Point of Entry in that it lasts five minutes and tells people about the past, present, and future of the organization. It clearly conveys the "gap" between where your organization is now and where you need to go in order to fulfill the next phase of your mission. Usually, the Visionary Leader Talk at the Ask Event highlights any new programs or accomplishments of the past year that were possible thanks to the prior year's contributions. This talk is delivered with emotion.

Video (Seven Minutes)
A video is essential at your Ask Event. We refer to this as a seven-minute, "three-cry" video. This is because the main job of the video

is to inspire people about the human impact of your work and move them to tears three times. It brings to light, in an emotional way, the deeper work of the organization. People should be noticeably moved, not necessarily because they feel sad or upset, but because they have been touched. Perhaps the video made them laugh or reminded them of all they have to be thankful for. First and foremost, the video must move people.

Most groups err on the side of too little emotion, feeling it is unprofessional or in some way insulting to the people they serve or the work they do. However, emotion is so essential to fundraising that most people are not even conscious of the degree to which their emotions drive their charitable giving. If you don't capture people's hearts as well as their minds, you will never have lifelong donors.

While there will be several other emotional aspects of the Ask Event program, including the Visionary Leader Talk and the testimonials, your program must also include a powerful, succinct, emotionally riveting, seven-minute (or shorter) video shown on a large screen in a big room with the lights turned down. People will feel the impact right in their chairs.

Testimonials (Six Minutes)

There is no substitute for a live testimonial. A firsthand account of how your organization changed a life is the most powerful statement of the impact of your work. It must leave people so deeply moved and reminded of what is truly important in life that they feel compelled to take action.

We allow a maximum of six minutes for the testimonial(s) at the Ask Event. There are several options for how to use this time. Most groups have one or, at the most, two Testimonial Speakers. The ideal Testimonial Speaker is someone who has had a firsthand experience of your organization's work—a client or family member, a longtime arts lover, a graduate of your school or program, etc.

The testimonial talk follows a prescribed outline with three main parts: what life was like before this person became involved with the organization, what services or intervention the organization offered that changed things for this person, and what life is like now, including how this person is able to give back to others.

You will need to script and rehearse your Testimonial Speakers to be sure they speak passionately and stay within their allocated time.

Pitch (Seven Minutes)

The Ask Event culminates in the pitch. It is now fifty minutes into the sixty-minute program. People have been warned that this is coming. They know they are going to be asked for money. At this point, 40%–50% of the people are ready to give. They want to know how to go about making a financial contribution right now. The remaining 50%–60% of the people are not ready to give at the event. They may end up giving the next day, the next week, or the next year. They may want to go home and talk it over with others, come to a Point of Entry themselves, transfer money or property, or meet with the board or committee. Or they may decide not to get involved with your organization at all. They may have other issues they are more involved with at this time.

The job of the Pitch Person at the Ask Event, then, is not to try to further persuade or convince people to give. The program has been sufficiently persuasive up to this point. The job of the Pitch Person is to focus on the people who are ready to give and to tell them how to go about doing that. The Pitch Person needs to be credible, in that they are genuinely connected to your mission, and they must be willing to follow the script. They understand that their job is to walk people through the pledge card and help them to give. They understand that they have a very specific and critical job to do.

The Pitch Person tells the Table Captains when to pass out the pledge cards, envelopes, and pens to each guest. After walking the audience through each line on the pledge sheet, instructing them how to fill out the form and giving them time to do that, the Pitch Person directs the guests to pass their envelopes back to the Table Captains.

The Table Captains have another essential role during the pitch. They must set the example for their guests by filling out their pledge cards at this time. Even if the Table Captains have already made a financial contribution to the organization, they need to be writing something on their pledge cards during the pitch. The guests will glance at the Table Captains and follow their lead.

See page 72 for a pledge card template.

Wrap Up (One Minute)
The emcee or board chair thanks everyone for coming and supporting the organization. People are invited to linger and chat if they like. The background music comes on, and the event ends, right on time, in sixty minutes.

Rehearsing
To improve the likelihood that your program will flow smoothly and each element will be strong and effective unto itself, it is essential to have a full rehearsal of the event program one to three days prior to the event, in the actual location where the event will take place.

CONVERTING EXISTING EVENTS INTO ASK EVENTS

As tempting as it may be to try to convert your lunch or dinner awards banquet or your auction gala into a Benevon Ask Event ("After all, we have been doing this other event for years, we have all of our loyal supporters right there, and we would raise so much more money if we could convert it into an Ask Event"), I have never seen it work.

The main reason I caution against converting any existing event into an Ask Event is that it will confuse and potentially anger your existing donors. The last thing you want to have happen in this process is for your donors to become upset with you. It is easy to assume, at first glance, that the Benevon Ask Event is just another variation on a traditional fundraising event. In fact, it is fundamentally different in three ways.

The first fundamental difference—which is invisible to most people—is the way that people are invited to the Ask Event. Guests are invited word-of-mouth by a friend who is truly passionate about the work of the organization and has agreed to be a Table Captain.

Unlike other fundraising events where the table hosts may represent businesses who have agreed to "sponsor" a table and underwrite the costs of the meal for their guests, Table Captains at the Ask Event have not paid anything to attend the event. Rather than needing to fill a pre-paid table with willing and hungry souls, the job of the Table Captain at the Ask Event is to invite people who have already attended Point of Entry Events or would be good candidates to attend them in the future. In other words, the passion of the Table Captain for your mission and the personal connection between the Table Captains and their guests are the key.

I used the word "anger" advisedly. As you likely know if you are already involved with fundraising events, people become very attached to these events. The events can begin to take on the personality of the superstar event chair, which is clearly not sustainable. We want to know that our groups will be putting on Ask Events (and Point of Entry Events and Free Feel-Good Cultivation Events) for as long as the organization is in existence. People should be coming to this event not because they want a nice night out or a good lunch or dinner, but because they care so much about the mission of your organization.

The second difference is that there is no ticket price to attend—it is truly free to all the guests. A ticket price is intentionally not a part of our model. People assume that if they have paid $150 to attend a "fundraising event," they have already given! By making the event free and telling people in advance that they do not have to give at all, guests subconsciously feel they can choose to give if they like.

The third difference is that there is no minimum and no maximum gift, and because the giving levels are relatively high (starting at $1,000 a year for each of the next five years, and going up from there), there will be fewer people who choose to give at an Ask Event than at a traditional event. However, those people who do give at these higher levels choose to do so of their own will (not out of guilt or obligation). They have been educated and inspired and truly want to contribute to the good work of the organization.

These are the fundamental differences in the Benevon Model, which are easy to miss if you merely substitute this event format for a prior fundraising event. The context of our model is permission and abundance. We believe that people truly want to give when they find causes that touch their hearts. There is no need to artificially force the process. It will happen very naturally in due course if you follow each step of the model.

Rather than tell you some of the scary stories about "converted Ask Events," I would advise the following: if you are excited about the Ask Event and would like to try it, begin the entire Benevon process, one step at a time, starting with the Point of Entry Events, leading up to a smaller, separate Ask Event the first year, while still putting on your other fundraising events. Although this will clearly be more work, in the long run it will be much less confusing to people and it will mark the whole process as separate and distinct from anything you are now doing. That way, down the road a year or two, once you have the proven financial results that the Benevon Model can produce for your organization, it will be far easier to stop doing your prior event(s) altogether and grow your Ask Event.

Now we are ready to move on to the third type of event, the Free Feel-Good Cultivation Event.

CHAPTER 8

FREE FEEL-GOOD CULTIVATION EVENTS

The third type of Benevon event is the Free Feel-Good Cultivation Event, also known as a Point of Re-Entry Event.

The purpose of the Free Feel-Good Cultivation Event is to recognize and appreciate the donors who have joined your Multiple-Year Giving Society and to give your organization an opportunity to connect face-to-face with each of your bigger donors at least twice a year.

Free Feel-Good Cultivation Events are not optional in the Benevon Model. They are essential to deepening your relationships with your donors. These recognition events are aimed at prior donors to reward them for their support and to reconnect them to their passion for your work. In our model, they must be free. If you find an underwriter to cover the costs of your annual mission-focused donor recognition event, it can become a Free Feel-Good Cultivation Event.

Many of the recognition or awards "feel-good" events you may already be putting on will fall into this category, especially if you find a sponsor to underwrite the costs of the event and then carefully "missionize" the content, inserting a brief program element that powerfully reconnects the donors to the mission of the organization, thereby serving as a Point of Re-Entry and reinforcing their original decision to give. Free Feel-Good Cultivation Events are not merely free, entertainment-style events. Donors do not pay to attend a *Free* Feel-Good Cultivation Event, nor is anyone asked to give at these events. These events must be related to your organization's mission.

Donors are encouraged to invite "new" people to these events. These will be people who have been hearing good things about your organization. Often they are precisely the kinds of people you would love to have attend your traditional Point of Entry Events but have been unable to find a way to invite them. For these new guests, the Free Feel-Good Cultivation Event is not a true Point of Entry, since the program will likely be shorter and more narrowly focused than a classic Point of Entry. But the spirit of the organization will no doubt be present, and the passion of the existing donors will be palpable to newcomers, so the odds are that when you call them to follow up and invite them to a Point of Entry, they will be delighted to attend.

The best Free Feel-Good Cultivation Events are program-related events that you are already doing, preceded by a reception for donors. The events that will have the best attendance are the ones that are a bit more special and exclusive (which does not necessarily mean smaller and more expensive).

For example, at the urban Christian school in Seattle where the model got started, we invited all of our Multiple-Year Giving Society Donors to a special reception just prior to the graduation ceremony each year. The graduation itself was a "full box of Kleenex affair." But the reception added a special touch. The guests felt honored to be among 200 or more top donors to the school who had each "sponsored" one or more students.

The brief program during the reception included a three-minute talk from the head of the school, who beamed with pride as he told of the successes of the students—test scores, which high schools they would be attending the next year, and special memories. Following his remarks, the donors heard from a grandmother and her grandson who was in the graduating class. They spoke with deep gratitude for what the school had provided, given the many other paths this young man could have taken.

The best Free Feel-Good Cultivation Events should make the donors feel that they are having an intimate fireside chat with someone very special and are among the first to hear the news. Your CEO should speak frankly about the real challenges the organization is facing now and into the future. After all, these are your organization's most loyal supporters. They did not sign on just to hear the good news. Your organization is doing the work that they are passionate about, so they are hungry for this openness and want to help you. This frank sharing of concerns tells your donors that they are part of a special, highly valued, "insider" group of people who your organization is so grateful to have.

You should plan to put on at least two Free Feel-Good Cultivation Events per year. One should be targeted to your highest Multiple-Year Giving Society Donors. Perhaps this event will be in a lovely home or be a light soup and salad dinner in your soup kitchen after it closes for the day. But it is for a smaller, targeted group of donors. The second event can be larger and for all your Multiple-Year Giving Society Donors, usually related to a pre-existing program event, like a camp visiting day or science fair. You can also have a third event for all of your donors.

Existing speaker series, special guest speakers, or briefings from the CEO also provide excellent occasions for Free Feel-Good Cultivation Events. A medical research group invites the top researcher to address the donors. A national expert in child abuse speaks to donors at a child abuse agency. Being invited to a brief reception before these presentations—with an opportunity to hear from the speaker and the other key people involved with the organization, including a brief testimonial from a client or service recipient—is compelling and once again provides that Point of Re-Entry element.

Of course, don't forget to do the critical one-on-one follow-up after each of these Free Feel-Good Cultivation Events. That is when the donors can tell you their next dreams for your organization, asking what more "we" can do together moving forward.

FREE FEEL-GOOD CULTIVATION EVENTS TO LAUNCH A CAMPAIGN

Free Feel-Good Cultivation Events are the right place in our model to test out and launch your next campaign—be it for major gifts, capital, or endowment—by spinning the next dream. They make wonderful informal focus group opportunities where you can share your plans and ask for advice and input from your insider group of loyal donors before you go public in a more formal way. They can be held in the executive director's office as a box lunch or at a private room in a restaurant or club.

Again, at our school in Seattle, we had several Point of Re-Entry Events right at our run-down school building, where we showed people the architect's drawings of the new building we wanted and told them about the costs involved. We ended up raising over $3 million for our capital campaign from eighteen of our existing Multiple-Year Giving Society Donors who had come to those Point of Re-Entry Events. Just like at a classic Point of Entry, you never ask for money at these events. You make the Follow-Up Call, determine the person's level and area of interest in the project, and proceed to cultivate them individually, leading up to a one-on-one Ask to support your major gifts, capital, or endowment fund.

CONVERTING EXISTING EVENTS TO FREE FEEL-GOOD CULTIVATION EVENTS

Let's look at some examples of events you might already be doing that you could convert into Free Feel-Good Cultivation Events.

Donor Recognition Event

The donor recognition reception or dinner is the classic example of a Free Feel-Good Cultivation Event. Many groups already put on this type of an annual event, but they may not think to insert all of these program elements.

Here is how this might work:

All donors at a certain giving level are invited to a special home, boat, or garden where they are thanked, honored, and reconnected to the facts and emotional impact of your work. They have been told in advance there will be a short program.

Begin with a welcome and thank you from one of your key board members. Plaques may be presented to each donor or something more personal, such as a child's framed drawing. Then be sure to include at least one live testimonial from a client, family member, volunteer, or staff member—someone authentic and articulate with a great story to tell (which you will already have had them write up and rehearse for you).

Next, the Visionary Leader briefs the donors on the state of the organization for no more than five minutes, telling them how far the organization has come thanks to their help. Then the Visionary Leader paints the picture of the organization's future, the next phase of the dream, and the next level of needs. This can border on a "soft" Ask. "We're looking forward to building our own building in the next three years. You'll be hearing more about that as the time comes closer." And be sure to ask: "How does this all sound to you?"

The Visionary Leader can even mention a Challenge Gift that has been received or, better yet, announce the challenge now to these donors as insiders. If the donors to the Challenge Gift Fund are present, have them say what inspired them to contribute in this way. It will help launch the next phase of the campaign and encourage people to increase their gifts. It is fine to have the Visionary Leader or board member say, "We are still looking for other gifts to be added to our Challenge Fund." That way no one will feel left out.

Notice all this is strictly informational. No one is being asked for money. After all, these donors are your inside family. If you were part of the family, you would not want to hear about this big news indirectly. You would want to be among the first to know. Perhaps you would have an opinion about it.

With your loyal donors, the issue is not when and how to ask them for money, but making sure you don't offend them by inadvertently overlooking them in some way. This is where your ongoing follow-up pays off. Someone knows those donors well enough to be able to anticipate how the program at your Free Feel-Good Cultivation Event will sound to them. It is as if you could do a dress rehearsal of the event and know how everyone in the audience will receive and interpret the information.

The entire program for this event should last no more than thirty minutes. Then give people plenty of time to mix and mingle and enjoy their meal. The networking effect of these events is magical. Be sure the crowd is interspersed with board and staff members who can give you feedback on each guest the next day. Since this is a Point of Re-Entry Event, you will be starting the cycle with your donors again by making Follow-Up Calls.

Regularly Scheduled Program Event
Another type of Free Feel-Good Cultivation Event is inviting your existing donors to a regularly scheduled program event such as a reunion with parents and premature babies hosted every other year by the neonatal unit at a major community hospital. It is preceded by a special reception for donors with the head physician in the pediatrics unit and the head of the hospital, filled with stories (from some of the families in attendance) and a tour of the new neonatal intensive care unit. Donors are invited to stay for the afternoon to meet the families and hear their stories.

Reception Preceding an Annual School Event
The annual cycle of school events offers many opportunities for Free Feel-Good Cultivation Events. A donor and board reception preceding the school holiday pageant, art show, or science fair would qualify nicely. Start with a welcome from a board member and the principal. Then have a proud teacher of the music, art, or science students tell a heartwarming student story to let guests know the difference their donations have made. Follow this with a testimonial from a grateful student who is planning to pursue a career in that field.

Forum with a Sought-After Speaker
Another example of a Free Feel-Good Cultivation Event is a private, issue-oriented forum with a sought-after speaker. This works well for policy and national organizations and can be taken on the road. Just be sure to include enough emotion in the testimonials and the impassioned dream of the Visionary Leader. Otherwise you will have an intellectual evening, which is not sufficient for a Free Feel-Good Cultivation Event (and people will not want to return your Follow-Up Calls).

A One-on-One Free Feel-Good

Another example is what we might call the One-on-One Free Feel-Good. An example might be inviting a major donor to meet one-on-one with a grateful student whose education was made possible thanks to a scholarship from this donor or a one-on-one lunch for a major donor and the medical researcher who will most benefit from her contribution to that laboratory research.

Trips and Missions

The best Free Feel-Good Cultivation Event of all is experiential, such as a live mission trip. Delivering boxes of food, providing medical relief, or helping build housing in developing countries provides a direct connection to the organization's purpose and a life-changing, firsthand experience. Anyone fortunate enough to go on one of these trips is likely to become a long-term supporter and a true believer in the cause. Be sure to follow up with each of these visitors and include them as speakers at subsequent Point of Entry Events and local Free Feel-Good Cultivation Events, such as the next example, the Free Feel-Good in a Box.

Free Feel-Good in a Box

We have one international relief group, based in Ohio, that noticed that most of their major donors went south for the winter. Rather than try to overcome that challenge, they took the Free Feel-Good to Florida and had it hosted by one of their major donor couples in their magnificent home. Their program consisted of a "spin the next dream" talk from their CEO, followed by a Testimonial Speaker—one of the donors right there in Florida—who had been on one of the mission trips.

Connecting National Donors to Local Needs

After Hurricane Katrina, one of our wonderful American Red Cross chapters in Louisville, Kentucky, put a great spin on a Free Feel-Good to connect local Katrina donors to the long-term local needs of their chapter. They invited their prior donors to a special event to hear from Louisville residents who had gone to New Orleans as Red Cross volunteers after Hurricane Katrina. These volunteers had quite a story to tell. In addition to the horrific scenes they had witnessed, they got very emotional about their pride for the work of the Red Cross. They each said they feared if a similar disaster were to befall Louisville, the city would likely not be prepared. They came back more resolved than ever to help their local Red Cross chapter increase its disaster response capacity. This greatly inspired local donors, many of whom stepped up their giving the next year.

Other Existing and Recurring Program Events
There is no need to cook up a brand-new event to have a Free Feel-Good Cultivation Event. What are some of the recurring program events that you are already doing that could be converted to Free Feel-Good Cultivation Events? Take a look at the list of events that you made earlier. Include those seemingly dry, internal training events, like training the core group of CPR instructors to teach others or tutoring lessons in the hallway of the after-school program or the graduation from your English as a Second Language school. These are moving and inspiring events that give your donors a sneak peek at your work and will make them want to give more and invite others to learn about your organization.

ATTENDANCE AT FREE FEEL-GOOD CULTIVATION EVENTS
Finally, let's look at some tips to ensure high attendance at your Free Feel-Good Cultivation Events, which can sometimes be a challenge. If you have adopted the Benevon Model, your goal should be to have each Multiple-Year Giving Society Donor attend two Free Feel-Good Cultivation Events per year. How well does your attendance measure up?

Here are some things to consider:

1. Do you know your donors well enough to know what they each need to feel special? "Special" means something different to each donor. One size does not fit all. The beautiful weeknight dinner may be just the wrong thing for the busy working couple with young children. They may prefer the Saturday night pre-concert reception instead. With a bit more thought, your hard work will be rewarded.

2. Does the event really make your donors feel good? Is the type of event, the timing, and the venue suitable to the majority of your donors? It is best to keep it simple and experiment. The fact that, "We've always done the annual dinner," doesn't mean it is what most of your donors want. If your attendance is dwindling, the event may have earned a reputation as being long, boring, inconvenient, etc.

3. Ask a few of your key donors—the ones you would most want to have attend—what they would like. Give them a few specific options to choose from. Many may say they would prefer a smaller, more intimate dinner in someone's home with the Visionary Leader or other star speaker. Others may prefer a daytime or weekend event where they can bring their family members to learn more about the organization or undertake some sort of volunteer project together. This qualifies as a Free Feel-Good Cultivation Event! Planning several smaller, low-budget events gives donors options.

4. Consider a One-on-One Free Feel-Good for some donors. There is no substitute for a meeting between the grateful scholarship recipient and the donor, or a meeting with the head of the literacy program and one of the former students who is now a volunteer.

5. Is the event mission-focused enough? Entertainment is no longer the big draw for most donors. Their time is too precious, and if they want to be entertained, they probably have their own favorite restaurant or cultural event to attend. The program at your Free Feel-Good Cultivation Event will be central to their decision to attend. Does it reconnect them to the mission and, even more specifically, to the aspect of the mission they are most passionate about? If your organization is working to cure a particular disease, will the speaker at the event be talking about the strain of the disease this donor is most interested in? This is the decision-making process your donors go through. Their time is limited, and they want to be sure they will get the greatest return for the time they give you.

6. Consider how people are being invited. These days, if you are truly expecting anyone to attend, the invitation must be highly personal. By our definition, "most personal" means a one-on-one phone call from someone they know and respect, not even a printed invitation with a handwritten note. If you cannot use this "most personal" approach, you can use the now familiar, but less personal note written on a pretty printed invitation, followed up with a phone call or an e-mail, from more than one person who the donor respects and knows personally. Anything short of that is not personal enough, and the donor will beg off as being too busy. You may even need to offer to provide transportation for people who are reluctant to drive or go out at night.

7. Finally, do not expect to bat 1,000. Even after all of your planning, one sick child, a snowy night, or an unexpected business trip can foil the best of intentions that donor may have had to attend. Just be sure to follow up individually with those absent guests who had confirmed that they would be there, to let them know that they were missed and to provide

them with the emotional essence of the event—for example, a lunch with the head of the oncology unit or a meeting with the principal of the school for a personal update. Making the effort to schedule something special just for them will communicate how important they are to you. Even if they can't make it, they will get the message.

Now we are ready to move from Free Feel-Good Cultivation Events to the fourth and final type of event: the Point of Entry Conversion Event.

CHAPTER 9

POINT OF ENTRY CONVERSION EVENTS

Point of Entry Conversion Events are your traditional, entertainment-style fundraising events—such as galas, golf outings, and auctions—after they have been "missionized" to include an inspiring Visionary Leader Talk, a Testimonial Speaker, and a method for capturing the names of those people who would like to come to a true Point of Entry.

In the Benevon Model, Point of Entry Conversion Events are entirely optional. There is no need to have them at all. When we work with newer nonprofits or groups that have not already been putting on these traditional fundraising events, we never suggest that they add them to their System of Events.

Once an organization fully adopts the Benevon Model and becomes focused intently on achieving sustainable funding, they recognize that it is their responsibility to connect each donor or potential donor to their mission in some way during each contact—whether one-on-one or at a group event. This means that each event must include a firsthand experience with the mission that people will never forget and a process for following up with everyone who expresses interest in learning more or becoming more involved. Because that is precisely what the three main events of the model—the Point of Entry, the Ask Event, and the Free Feel-Good Cultivation Event—are designed to accomplish, most groups find no need to include any other types of events in their repertoire.

Some groups that join our program are already overloaded with special events. We work with them to either missionize each event, convert it to a different type of event within the Benevon Model, or phase it out altogether. For example, we might recommend that a group ask a loyal sponsor to underwrite the costs of the annual holiday donor appreciation dinner so the group can convert it into a Free Feel-Good Cultivation Event. Or we might encourage them to have a group of volunteers put on the event privately (i.e., *they* do all the work) and present the organization with a check for the proceeds!

If an event must stay on the list, we help groups missionize the format and articulate the specific benefits of the event, including the financial benefits. If an event accesses a different part of the social or geographic community, reaches more corporate donors, or just needs to stay for political reasons, infusing it with new life and doing rigorous follow-up with the people who give permission for it can justify keeping the event on your list, at least for another year.

We have learned, over time, that each special event comes fraught with its own "special" emotional and political baggage. The habitual default to, "It's time for the annual auction again," often blinds smart board and staff members to the enormous opportunity cost of using precious staff time for making centerpieces rather than cultivating donors.

Once you become clearly focused on the work of building sustainable funding and seeing the fruits of your labor, you will likely join the ranks of the many groups that have liberated themselves entirely from their dependence on these off-purpose fundraising social events, or you will see how to convert these events into something more productive. In other words, if you are serious about building sustainable funding, you should have a plan and clear timeline for missionizing/converting or—ideally—phasing out each of these events as soon as possible.

At the school in Seattle where the model got started, the only fundraising event we ever did was our annual Ask Event. All of the remaining time in the year was spent on two things. First, the systematic, personal cultivation of our Multiple-Year Giving Society Donors to engage them in whichever aspect of our work most interested them. That is why so many of our donors paid off their five-year pledges early or chose to increase their giving to the school. We did not have time to be planning more parties. Working with donors one-on-one generated far more money than any special event—other than our Ask Event, which was a one-hour showcase of our mission. Second, we focused on putting on sizzling Point of Entry Events as often as needed to accommodate all the referrals from our prior donors and Point of Entry guests.

CONVERTING EXISTING FUNDRAISING EVENTS INTO POINT OF ENTRY CONVERSION EVENTS

The true test of a successful conversion event is whether or not, the day after the event, every guest will remember the name of your organization and have an idea about how your organization is changing the world. This is not difficult to accomplish if you plan these elements right into your event timeline.

Golf Tournament

Let's take something pretty standard like a golf tournament, although this same formula could be adapted to any fundraising event. Unlike a Point of Entry Event, where people know they have been invited to an introductory educational session about the work of the organization, people coming to a golf tournament are coming to play golf.

What people will remember most is a story. The best way to accomplish this is to insert a brief Point of Entry element into the program while people are seated, having dinner or lunch. This can be accomplished easily with a five-minute Visionary Leader Talk plus a three-minute live testimonial. At a golf tournament or other entertainment or sports event, you only have enough permission to insert a brief program about your work. After all, people really came because they wanted to play golf, watch the game, or enjoy the dinner.

Here is an example of how you could missionize a golf tournament: While everyone is seated at the lunch or dinner after the tournament, the emcee or board chair gets up and says, "We know most of you came today for a great day of golf, and we hope you've had that. As you know, today's event is a benefit for (organization), and we here at (organization) would not be doing our jobs if we did not take advantage of having you all gathered here today to tell you a little more about the work we do at (organization)."

Then have your Visionary Leader speak for three minutes, including a personal story about why they do the work they do or what keeps them there. Follow this with a powerful, three-minute live testimonial from a recipient of your services or a family member.

Following the testimonial, the emcee gets back up and thanks the Testimonial Speaker.

"Now that you have learned a little more about what we do here at (organization), some of you may find that you'd like to learn more about our work firsthand or just be kept informed about what we're doing. In that case, there's a card under your plate (or inserted in your program) and pens in the center of the table for you to fill out the card and give it to your table host."

As they are looking for the cards and filling them in, the emcee continues:

"If you have been moved and inspired by the messages you have heard here today, we would love to have you come to our (Point of Entry) tour at (organization). This is a one-hour dynamic tour that goes into more depth about our work and some of the stories of the people we serve. I've taken the tour, and I will say—it was incredible. As a board member, even I didn't realize all the different things that (organization) is doing in our community. You may also be interested in other parts of our work. We'd be happy to talk with you about those ideas too. I really encourage you to join us for a tour. We will not contact you unless you give us your permission to do so by filling out one of these cards today. We hope that you have been inspired by the information presented here today."

Train the people who will be collecting the cards to be very upbeat and gracious with the people at their table. They can say something that is "inviting" to their table to make it easy for people to fill out the cards. While we know that not everyone will fill out this card, the encouragement from the person at the podium and the people serving as their table hosts will help.

If it is an evening event where people often don't have their business cards with them, put a preprinted card in the brochure, under each plate, or in the center of the table for interested guests to fill out and give to the table host.

Those people who give you cards are the only ones with whom you have enough permission to follow up, invite to a Point of Entry Event, and take around the cycle.

Black-Tie Awards Dinner

A participant in one of our workshops did this brilliantly at a black-tie dinner "fundraiser" that honored formerly homeless women who had turned their lives around. The tables had been sold to corporate sponsors, many of whom had given their tickets away to others to fill up the tables.

The development director assumed that although the guests were there primarily to attend a lovely dinner, the organization could take ten minutes to tell them about its work. They started the program with some inspirational words from the emcee, the CEO of the major corporate sponsor of the event. This was followed immediately by a moving video about the organization's work.

Then the emcee encouraged people to enjoy their dinner and spend some time talking with the special guest at their table who was most familiar with the organization—either a board member, volunteer, or staff person. He also encouraged them to take a moment to read the testimonial inserts in their printed programs.

After dinner came the well-scripted awards presentations. This portion of the program served as a real-life testimonial to the extraordinary accomplishments of these women in the face of great obstacles. As each woman was called up to receive her award, she was asked to sit in one of the chairs on the stage. At the end of the awards, all the recipients were asked to stand. Of course, after hearing each woman's story, there was a standing ovation and not a dry eye in the house.

Board members were assigned clusters of tables to visit after the dessert was served. The executive director had briefed the table hosts on the overall objective for the event. "This isn't just a pretty party. We want to be sure every single guest leaves here tonight knowing more about our organization, both the facts and the emotional impact of the work we do." Table hosts, staff, and board members all knew in advance that the development staff would be calling them to debrief on Monday morning. They knew to be on the lookout for people who expressed a real interest in the cause. And they knew that, before the evening ended, the emcee would invite the guests to leave their business card or let their table host know if they would like more information about the organization.

Within a week, every guest who expressed any sincere interest in the organization had received a Follow-Up Call from the development director. This was in addition to the standard thank-you call or note that their table host would do.

Many people asked if they could take a tour of the shelter (which became their real Point of Entry Event). Others offered in-kind or cash gifts. Some wanted to host a Point of Entry Event of their own. Because this organization was planning to do a Free One-Hour Ask Event a few months later, they were able to convert many of the black-tie dinner guests into Table Captains for the upcoming Ask Event. The organization raised more than $300,000 at this black-tie gala Point of Entry Conversion Event, as well as generating the passion and commitment that led to many new Table Captains for their bigger Ask Event. Good strategy!

Annual Bridge Tournament and Luncheon

Thanks to Karen Wildfoerster, development director, and her team at Alliance House in Salt Lake City for providing this firsthand account:

> *We realized that the great majority of the 150 or so ladies who attended our bridge tournament every year had very little idea of what Alliance House actually does. We decided to eliminate the silent auction and raffle, raise the registration fee by $15, and add a ten-minute program. Our executive director spoke about the mission and philosophy of Alliance House, then introduced one of our members (clients) who gave a very articulate and truly moving account of her life with mental illness and what Alliance House has done for her. She received a standing ovation from the ladies.*

From the time the social hour began at 11:30 a.m. through the end of the bridge playing at 3:30 p.m. (with the exception of the program, which also included an annual award we give out), we had a slide show going with pictures of our staff and members in a variety of activities, intermingled with powerful mental health facts and statements.

To capture the names with people's permission, at each table, we placed cards and pens (one per person), thanking them for their interest in Alliance House, with space for their name, address, phone number, e-mail, and comments.

At the end of the program portion of the lunch, one of our board members, who knows many of the ladies well, pointed out the cards and asked everyone to fill them out if they would like more information or a tour of Alliance House. She let them know that we would be coming around later to pick up the cards.

For our follow-up, within a week of the event, we called each of the eighteen ladies who filled out an information card and asked for their feedback on the event and invited them for a tour. We encouraged them to invite someone else to come along—a spouse, neighbor, friend, or bridge partner—for the tour.

Also, because we eliminated the silent auction and raffle after so many years, we called a few of our loyal, frequent attendees who did not fill out a card to ask how they felt about the change in the event. Did they miss having the auction or raffle? How did they feel about having the speakers? We already knew that many of the ladies actually found the raffle and auction somewhat annoying, so we didn't anticipate having many complaints. For most of these ladies, I listened to their feedback and thanked them. For others who expressed more interest, I asked them if they'd like to come for a tour.

One interesting anecdote: one of the ladies stopped to tell me that she had never actually made a donation to Alliance House before (except her registration fee for this event), but after hearing our speaker, she planned to write a check. Most of the comments I heard about our speaker were very positive.

I heard from board members who attended that at least half a dozen women commented that they were glad the lengthy auction and raffle had been eliminated. The event had cost $50 for the previous nine years and in this, the tenth year, we raised it to $65. I did not hear of a single complaint.

Since we no longer had to spend hours and hours looking for raffle prizes and auction items, we solicited just a handful of businesses for higher value gifts and gave them as door prizes in a drawing. People seemed excited at the prospect of winning one of these more valuable prizes, and the winners were very pleased.

One thing I would say to other groups considering modifying or converting an existing event into a Benevon-style Point of Entry Conversion Event is, don't be afraid of change! If you have a mediocre event that takes more of your time and effort than it is worth, yet it is a popular event, figure out how to change it to make it more worth your time and effort!

Chili Cook-Off

Any fun, large-scale event—like the annual Chili Cook-Off, which includes about four hours of cooking competition and entertainment—can be converted to a Point of Entry Conversion Event. Once you have refined your message, focusing on the three main areas of your work, the myth-buster facts, and the compelling stories and needs associated with each area, you can weave these throughout the Visionary Leader Talk and your live Testimonial Speaker during your ten-minute program while everyone is seated.

The biggest challenge at a "mill-around," festival-type event like this is selecting or crafting the best time for the program to take place. People must be seated during the program. At a chili cook-off, no doubt there will be a time for judging the best chili and announcing the winners. At that point, everyone will likely be seated, eating their chili. That would be the time for your program!

Can you see how easy it would be, in the absence of such a program, for the guests to leave the event having had a wonderful time, yet unaware of the name of the organization benefiting from this event or the purpose of the organization? Because these large-scale public events tend to take a great deal more work than anyone ever imagines at the start, they also are wonderful candidates for "outsourcing." Namely, asking one of your volunteer groups or perhaps a church group that already supports your organization to put the event on for you and send you the check. In other words, you need to closely evaluate the cost/benefit ratio on putting on this type of event. Odds are, this will be an event to phase out, as soon as you get the Benevon Model producing solid results.

Bowl-a-Thon or Fun Run

Much like the large-scale chili cook-off, the large-scale "thon" events are great contenders for "missionization," conversion, and, in some cases, eventual elimination.

For our purposes here, let's assume you have done your cost/benefit analysis and decided that the event should continue for at least one more year. How, then, can you convert it to a Point of Entry Conversion Event?

First, you need to find the "sit-down" moments. Is there an orientation meeting for the runners, walkers, bowlers, or their team leaders? Why not have a meeting with those people prior to the event, perhaps a more social kickoff type of event, where you could have your ten-minute program? After all, the more inspired people are before they start raising the money to sponsor themselves in your race or "thon," the more money they are likely to raise. Use that kickoff meeting to have testimonials from one of last year's runners, one of last year's donors, and a client or family member who benefited from the programs these runners' funds allowed you to offer.

For added emotional impact, ask each runner or "thon-er" to tell you why they have chosen to participate in your event. What is their personal connection to your mission? How much would it mean to them to see that disease cured or that environmental issue handled?

On the day of the event, find a time when everyone is seated or could be seated. For example, when participants wait in line to sign in, you could have a tent or booth with chairs for them to take ten minutes to remind themselves what this is all really for. Offer some snack food in the tent, and you will have every seat filled. Put on these ten-minute mini-programs all day. If runners have numbers pinned to their shirts, you can ask them if it would be OK with them to use their runner's number to find their contact information so you can invite them to a real Point of Entry.

Another opportunity for a sit-down moment is the awards ceremony after the event, although not everyone will stay for that. If there is a banquet or other private event for certain superstar participants or volunteers, that could be another opportunity to present your ten-minute program. Each time, be sure to have a way to ask people who are interested to give you their contact information and let them know that you will be following up with them.

One group that we work with does an annual three-day bowling marathon. They do their mini-programs in the bar while people are waiting for their turn to bowl. They also have students who come around to each bowling lane to talk with the bowlers who are waiting for their turn.

After these events, some groups hold awards dinners or celebrations for the runners or bowlers who raised the most money for the nonprofit. Hopefully, by this point, most of these superstar runners/fundraisers will have attended a Point of Entry (some groups require that all participants attend a Point of Entry before they are accepted as runners, sometimes hosted at their worksites as Point of Entry Events in a Box) and be ready to get involved in a bigger way. These truly engaged "volunteers" make great Table Captains at your Ask Event, where they can host one or more tables of all the runners or bowlers who want to get more involved. These same "thon" participants often become the bigger donors at Ask Events, making five-year pledges to the Multiple-Year Giving Society, because they so appreciate the work of the organization.

Before we move on from the "thon" event, consider again the high cost of producing this event—including both staff and volunteer time. Is it really worth it? The only way to make these events sustainable, in my opinion, is to use them as a feeder for Point of Entry Events and subsequent Table Captains for your Ask Event, and ultimately, Multiple-Year Giving Society Donors. If not for that rigorous follow-up and tracking of every runner or participant, why have these events at all?

Auction

Like golf and galas, auctions are well entrenched into the life of many nonprofits. Here is an idea for how to convert your gala/auction, courtesy of Rodney Bivens and Damon King at the Regional Food Bank of Oklahoma.

> *Before we got started with Benevon, we were putting on many special events. They were our main source of fundraising. Now we just do two events—our Hope's Harvest (Ask Event) and one gala/auction event—our Chefs' Feast—which we feel we have successfully infused with our mission.*
>
> *Our Chefs' Feast gala had become one of the most popular events in our community, mostly because twenty-five top chefs from the finest restaurants in Oklahoma City set up gourmet food stations around the room, and for $100 per person, you can meet the chefs and eat all you want of their delicious creations. Corporations bought tables in advance and gave out the tickets to people as a special treat to have a nice evening out. Many of the guests had no prior firsthand knowledge of the work of the Food Bank.*
>
> *In the past, in addition to the food stations, we had a traditional silent and live auction during the sit-down portion of the evening, with guests placing bids on items we had spent a long time collecting. The items themselves took up a lot of room in the venue where we could have been seating more guests. After we began implementing the Benevon Model, we decided to consolidate these auctions into a single, mission-focused auction called Fund-a-Child. It is still an "auction," but instead of items, guests are invited to support our children's feeding programs by contributing*

at various levels.

We make sure the event connects people emotionally to our mission. From the moment guests walk through the door, everything they see is about our mission: the signage using our mission-driven tag lines—"Fighting Hunger...Feeding Hope," the shirts worn by our volunteers, and the pictures of our clients on the programs given to the guests. A large screen at the front of the room has a streaming PowerPoint presentation acknowledging our sponsors, interspersed with Food Bank facts, pictures, and stories of our food programs. Throughout the event, guests are reminded that every dollar raised will be used to feed hungry Oklahomans. During the program, our executive director speaks for five minutes, sharing the vision of the organization, stories of hope, and where we want to be in the future.

During the Fund-a-Child Auction, guests are invited to make a "bid" at various levels of support. At each level, guests are told what a gift of that amount will accomplish. For instance, a bid of $5,000 enables the Food Bank to provide 35,000 meals or thirty-seven backpacks of weekend food for an entire school year to chronically hungry elementary school children. The bid levels start at $10,000 (and we try to arrange a bid at that level in advance to announce as a challenge) and incrementally decline to $50. The bottom line is, regardless of their financial capacity, everyone is given the opportunity to make a difference in the life of a child.

After the event, we call each Fund-a-Child donor to thank them and to invite them to our Point of Entry. Our executive director calls all the donors at the highest levels.

The results have been excellent. Using the old format of dinner and live and silent auctions, we had netted an average of approximately $80,000 per year from the event. But that does not tell the real story of the number of hours our staff put into securing auction items, when they could have been doing other work. Using this new format, the overall gala brings in approximately $120,000 net, $30,000 to $50,000 *of which comes from the Fund-a-Child auction. Now that we have figured out how to have our two events peacefully coexist, we plan to keep them both. Many people attend both events, and they invite their friends to our Food for Thought (Point of Entry) tours all year long.*

Point of Entry Conversion Events as a Stalling Tactic
As tempting as it may be to convert an existing event, be sure you are not just prolonging the inevitable, for fear of having people upset with you for telling the truth about the misplaced energy required to produce this event. You may be the only person who is in a position to comment on that. Sometimes, your best legacy to an organization is telling the truth so they will stop doing something that is not productive.

FOLLOW-UP AFTER A POINT OF ENTRY CONVERSION EVENT

Whether you are trying to convert a golf tournament, a black-tie gala, a concert, or a picnic into a Point of Entry Conversion Event, remember that the third essential ingredient is to capture the names of those who want more information. No captured names means no Point of Entry Event guests. As you can see, these Point of Entry Conversion Events are far less efficient in terms of generating new potential donors than are the classic Point of Entry Events. At the classic Point of Entry, you generally have permission to follow up with everyone who has come and to continue around our circle model for as long as they express interest. At these conversion events, you can only follow up with the people who request follow-up, and, odds are, that will be less than 100% of the people in attendance.

Let's continue with a deeper look at event follow-up.

CHAPTER 10

POST-EVENT FOLLOW-UP

I suspect that, by now, you are getting a sense of the importance of follow-up in the Benevon Model. Follow-up is the glue that holds the model together.

PLANNING EVENTS: BEGIN WITH THE FOLLOW-UP

We tell our groups that if they are not planning to do systematic follow-up after each event, they should not have the event at all. Although it seems counterintuitive, the first thing to consider as you redesign each of your events to grow your base of lifelong donors is how you are going to manage the follow-up. This is true whether the event is destined to become a Point of Entry, a Free Feel-Good Cultivation Event, or a Free One-Hour Ask Event. You must plan the entire event working backwards from your follow-up plan. Think about what you want to hear people saying when you make those Five-Step Follow-Up Calls. What is it you most want them to remember about your organization? Is it the great auction item they bought or the story about the child saved thanks to your cutting-edge medical research? Then you can design your event to produce that kind of feedback.

Capturing the Names with Permission

In the Benevon Model, you can make Follow-Up Calls only to those people who have given you permission to do so. How will you decide which of the guests you can legitimately follow up with? How will you identify and record the names of the people who would like to stay in contact with you? How will they let you know that you have their permission to contact them?

The easiest and most up-front method is to have some sort of reply card that the guests can fill out and give back to a designated person, ideally their table host, indicating that they would like more information about your program. While this is clearly the most straightforward method, even those who are very interested may be reluctant to be the only person at their table who is filling out such a card.

Another approach that works well is to have the emcee, or some other key person who is part of the official program, say something like this after the Facts 101 and Emotional Hook have been presented:

"While we know that most of you just came today to play golf (or dance, etc.), you may have discovered during our program that you have an interest in learning more about our work. There is a person seated at each table who is very familiar with our organization. For today, they are serving as our experts. Would that person at each table please raise your hand now so we can all see who you are? (Pause while hands go up and everyone looks around.) Feel free to speak with them and let them know you'd like more information. We would be delighted to have someone from the organization speak with you further."

That kind of a statement sets you up pretty well to capture the next tier of interested guests.

Give these designated experts special ribbons on their name tags. Let them know in advance that you are counting on them to circulate and talk to as many people as they can during the event. Tell them you will be calling to debrief with them the day after the event. In other words, they should be on their toes during the entire event.

A third approach is to call those guests who were prior "insiders"—donors, volunteers, or board members—even though they may not have given you express prior permission to do so. I think it is safe to assume that, with them, you already have enough implicit permission to call them randomly and ask for their frank feedback about the event. Also ask them about any other comments or reactions they heard from other guests. They will be flattered that you consider them enough of an insider to call.

A fourth strategy is to review the various categories of guests in terms of their past association with your organization or in terms of the role they played in the event and then call two or three key people in each category to help you with your "random follow-up survey." While this may feel a bit contrived, people will be impressed that you are taking the time to solicit their input, and most will be delighted to talk to you. As you listen to their responses, see if you can sniff out any trends that you might want to pursue with a telephone or e-mail campaign to a broader group of attendees.

Lastly, consider the guests who said they wanted to attend but did not attend. How could you genuinely follow up with them? If a personal phone call seems like too much, could you send them a copy of the video with a "we missed you" note from their friend?

Everyone who will be involved in the follow-up process needs to be well-prepared from the beginning. They are your undercover agents during the event. Deputize your board members and long-term supporters. Have them keep their antennae up.

What Kind of Follow-Up and When?

Timing is critical to your follow-up strategy. The two weeks after each event is, by far, the most fertile time for additional fundraising and cultivation. For most event organizers, by the time the actual event happens, they are burned out and exhausted. Your guests, on the other hand, are just getting interested. Now is the time when they are curious and eager to learn more. Tell your event planners and key development staff not to schedule their vacations until at least two weeks after the event. Otherwise they miss this time-sensitive opportunity.

In terms of the type of follow-up, you have no doubt already thought of the obvious: letters. Most organizations have the thank-you letter down to an art form. It is a beautifully crafted letter, personally signed by the perfect person. Ideally suited to the pace of the old reality, it arrives two or three weeks after the event. By then, you will be lucky if your guests even remember having attended. In other words, in the new reality, letters are fine for the formal IRS-required response and for the lovely memento, especially if they are handwritten. But they will not get you that timely, open-ended feedback you need.

Your first choice should be the telephone because it provides immediate, voice-to-voice, real-time dialog. Although many of your donors may prefer e-mail, for the majority, nothing yet substitutes for a phone call or a voicemail message left within three days of the event, while the afterglow is still warm. This call or message thanks the person for coming and asks for their feedback, again engaging them directly with a real person associated with your organization.

Speaking of messages, yes, it is fine to leave a voicemail or send an e-mail message. Let them know how to reach you and be prepared to call them two more times to actually connect with them. One final message can be sent by e-mail.

All of this phone contact requires that you have been doing an impeccable job of capturing the names and phone numbers of the guests at your event. If the event was well done, the guests will have left inspired and educated. In other words, they should still remember you. Since many of them gave you their names to be called, they will be looking forward to hearing from you.

Who Is the Best Person to Make the Benevon Five-Step Follow-Up Call?

The best person to make the Follow-Up Call is someone very closely connected to your organization. Ideally, this person is someone the guest met at the event, even in passing, who will be their ongoing contact over the next few years. In many cases, this will be one high-level staff person or a longtime volunteer who single-handedly does all the follow-up. This provides consistency for your guests.

I do not recommend having guests receive the official Five-Step Follow-Up Call from a personal friend. While the friend can make a courtesy thank-you call, the official Follow-Up Call should be done by someone closer to the inside of the organization, yet at arms-length from the guests so the guests have the freedom to give direct and honest feedback.

The only exception to having just one insider make all the calls is in the case of a very large event where a large number of guests will be receiving Follow-Up Calls. Then you will need many callers. In this case, assemble your best team or train the table experts to make the Follow-Up Calls. Again, do not have people on your "call team" making these Follow-Up Calls to their friends.

SCRIPT FOR THE POST-EVENT BENEVON FOLLOW-UP CALL

Be sure that each caller is following the same script or outline of the general questions you want to have covered. This will ensure consistency. Also, be sure they have a standardized way of recording the information so it can be entered into your database right away.

Here is a basic script of what you will want to cover in the post-event Follow-Up Call. You will want to modify it to fit your situation.

1. Thank the person for coming to the event. Let them know your organization is honored that they made it a priority to be there.
2. Ask them what they thought about the event. What did they like most about it? Do they feel they learned anything new about the organization? What suggestions would they have for changes or improvements?
3. Is there any way they might like to become more involved with the organization? If they have already been involved, listen carefully here for signs of renewed or increased interest.
4. Is there anyone who came to mind during the event who they would suggest you contact or invite to a tour or other Point of Entry Event?
5. If they requested any additional information, let them know how you will be providing that. Thank them for taking their time for this call.

I'll end this chapter with an example of brilliant follow-up work done by the health sciences division of a large university we worked with. Any organization could adopt this approach.

The health sciences division had just completed raising over $200 million as part of a university-wide campaign raising $1 billion. This hospital brought Benevon in to do "backfill cultivation" of the recent major donors, fearing most of them had been strong-armed and pressured to give without having any personal or emotional connection to the intended outcome of their gift.

We designed a half-day, Saturday morning, high-end Free Feel-Good/Point of Re-Entry Event, showcasing the incredibly promising research of four scientists. The day began with a greeting from the chairman of the university's board of trustees, followed by a greeting from the chair of the health sciences division, who thanked people for their generous gifts to date.

Each guest had pre-registered to attend one of the four simultaneous breakout sessions with one of the scientists, depending on their area of interest—as I recall, one was working on brain research, one on breast cancer, one on juvenile diabetes, and one on arthritis.

The chair of the division encouraged people to ask questions in these presentations, to make the research relevant to them—to real people.

The scientists had all been coached to make their work understandable to lay people. They removed all the super-clinical slides and graphs and explained—in human terms—what they were doing, the results of clinical tests to date, and future studies planned. They showed people the impact of even incremental scientific discoveries. They talked about the new medicines that have been developed thanks to this research. Each presentation also included a testimonial from a grateful patient or family member.

The morning ended with a lunch in the elegant faculty dining room and a talk from the president of the university.

The very first step in planning this entire program with the division was to meet—about four months prior to the event—with all the staff who would be making the Follow-Up Calls after this "Super Saturday" (our internal code name) event. We carefully assigned the appropriate staff person to each of the four breakout rooms, reviewed the names of the guests who had registered to attend each session, and showed staff members the form that we wanted them to fill out after the event, documenting each conversation with a donor or potential donor (not everyone in attendance was a prior donor—as a Free Feel-Good Cultivation Event, donors were encouraged to invite others whom they felt might like to know more about what was going on behind that big gate at the university). In other words, staff knew—weeks in advance—which room they would be in and who they were to meet and talk to. In most cases, these staff members already were familiar with these donors and the particular research project being discussed. These same staff members would be "assigned" to these donors going forward, similar to a private banker at a bank or investment firm. We scheduled a meeting for the day after the event to debrief, share feedback, and compare notes.

The day of the event flowed like clockwork. The presentations came off brilliantly. The donors were inspired and engaged in what they heard and saw.

Three days later, the Follow-Up Calls began, also like clockwork. Following the script for the Benevon Follow-Up Call, each staff member asked the open-ended questions and listened closely to people's responses. Some wanted more information. Many said they had not stopped thinking about the researcher's own personal story about why they began seeking a cure for this particular disease in the first place. Some asked for another meeting to discuss the next research funding needs. Some offered to involve their friends, business colleagues, and associates at charitable foundations. All of the notes were entered into the department's confidential database. Overall, the event was a smashing success. Every bit of it flowed perfectly. Everyone who had been involved in producing the event felt a great sense of satisfaction about the relationships that had been strengthened and the trust that had been built out of that "Super Saturday" event.

And it had all been planned working backwards from the follow-up.

Now let's move on to designing your System of Events.

CHAPTER 11

DESIGNING YOUR SYSTEM OF EVENTS

Now that you understand the event classification within the Benevon Model and how the events you are currently producing could be missionized, let's revisit the ideal System of Events that you are aiming for. Then you can begin the process of crafting the ideal System of Events for your organization.

As you go through this process, think ahead all the way to your goal. What is the simplest, most streamlined and effective package of events that you could leave as a legacy for your organization? What are the most mission-focused events that could go on year after year, each time infused with new stories that educate and inspire?

For right now, do not be concerned about how you will get from here to there. Merely tell the truth about what "there" should look like. Think from the perspective of your organization's mission. Which package of events would most honor that mission, rather than hide it or cheapen it?

To repeat, the classic System of Events for organizations using the Benevon Model is:

- A minimum of one Point of Entry Event per month. Most groups settle in on one classic Point of Entry at their office or program site per month, plus one or two Point of Entry Events in a Box per month.
- One Ask Event per year.
- Two to three Free Feel-Good Cultivation Events per year. One is for your highest level Multiple-Year Giving Society Donors and the other is for all your Multiple-Year Giving

Society Donors. A third Free Feel-Good Cultivation Event is also recommended for all donors (not just those in your Multiple-Year Giving Society).

Note: There are zero Point of Entry Conversion Events or Pre-Point of Entry Events on this list.

Let's look now at the System of Events chart that you began in Chapter 4. Revisit and expand your list of current events in the first column. This list should include existing fundraising events as well as program events, classes for your participants and staff, volunteer-recruitment events, events to recruit blood donors, staff recognition parties, etc. Do not limit yourself to the obvious fundraising events only.

SYSTEM OF EVENTS

Current Events	Convert Event To:						Ideal Month	Add/ Convert/ Eliminate By When
	Pre-Point of Entry Event	Point of Entry Event	Point of Entry in a Box	One-on-One Point of Entry	Point of Entry Conversion Event	Free Feel-Good Cultivation Event		
1.								
2.								
3.								
4.								
5.								
6.								
7.								
8.								
9.								
10.								

Looking to the chart, which of your events are contenders to be converted to either a Point of Entry (or Point of Entry in a Box), a Point of Entry Conversion Event, or a Free Feel-Good Cultivation Event? (Remember that no existing event should be converted to a Benevon Ask Event.)

Which of these events are you now considering converting to become a classic Benevon Point of Entry in your office or program site? Which ones could become program elements or tour stops during your classic Point of Entry (for example, the job training or tutoring program which happens every Thursday)? Which events would best be converted to become Point of Entry Events in a Box, where you take your Point of Entry on the road to a venue that you "control"? Which ones need to be re-classified as Pre-Point of Entry Events, where you are invited to speak at another group's meeting? Which need to be "missionized" and turned into a Point of Entry Conversion Event? Tell the truth as you review your list. You are crafting your ideal lasting plan.

Do you have any events that are similar to an Ask Event? In other words, are you already doing some type of "ask event" that must be factored into your system going forward? Assuming that it cannot be converted into an Ask Event, what is the best way to maximize the goodwill and the financial return it brings you now? How can you win over the longtime supporters of that event to the merits of putting on a Benevon Ask Event? What else can you do with your existing "ask event" to preserve the spirit of it? Can you convert it to either a Point of Entry or Free Feel-Good Cultivation Event? If, in addition to asking for money during the event, people also pay a ticket price to attend, the event would be a good contender to become a Point of Entry Conversion Event.

Moving to Free Feel-Good Cultivation Events, what contenders do you have for that category? Do they have a heartfelt, mission-based program already built into them, such as a graduation ceremony from your English as a Second Language program or a homecoming reception to honor your overseas mission volunteers? Perhaps these are existing "fundraising" events, in that you sell tickets to attend them, like an annual volunteer recognition awards dinner. How can you get the cost of these events underwritten so they can now become free? You don't need to have more than two of these events, so don't overburden yourself here.

"BLESSING AND RELEASING" EVENTS

Let's look next at the events on your list that have not been selected for conversion thus far. These are the events that most likely need to be "blessed and released"—either gradually or immediately. These tend to be the fundraising events that are not even worth converting to Point of Entry Conversion Events because they do not reap enough in dollars or goodwill to justify the time and effort needed to produce them.

It is fine to have a sentimental moment of silence for each event as you "bless and release" it. While it may have served you well up to now, the time spent on putting on that beautiful event can now be used for follow-up and cultivation of people who have been educated and inspired about your work and have given you their express permission to keep contacting them after a Point of Entry, Ask Event, or Free Feel-Good Cultivation Event. This is the precious time you will need to cultivate these individuals personally. Many of them will become major donors. *In the long run, eliminating several events will allow you to grow a significant major gifts program, which is the missing steppingstone for most nonprofits that are serious about building sustainable funding.*

You may be surprised to see what a difference it will make just to check the box that says you are planning to eliminate an event. Just like when you "bless and release" a Point of Entry guest or a potential donor, paradoxically, new possibilities seem to open up. You may suddenly see many other ways to retain the best elements of the event (often by blending them into another event) without needing to keep the original event intact.

Or, as demonstrated in the following example, you may find a great community group that will take over hosting and producing the event and just invite you to speak as part of the event program, where they will present you with the check for the net proceeds of the event.

The Power of "Blessing and Releasing" a Cherished Special Event

Thanks to Kathleen Reynolds and Roseanne Brown at Generations Group Homes in Simpsonville, South Carolina, for sharing this excellent example of what can happen when an organization makes the decision to eliminate an event—in this case, a golf tournament.

After becoming part of the Benevon Curriculum for Sustainable Funding, we realized it was time to give up our seven-year-old golf tournament. Rather than eliminate it outright, we tried first to convert it to a Point of Entry Conversion Event, by inserting a Visionary Leader Talk and Testimonial Speaker at the dinner banquet following the day of golf to see if we would get Point of Entry referrals from the golfers. We were prepared to track all the referrals, but we didn't get a single one! We decided that if we couldn't make the golf day productive by getting anyone interested in coming to our Point of Entry Events or referring others, that we didn't have time for it, so we dropped it in order to be able to focus on the other aspects of the model.

Initially, we sent out an e-mail update telling the golfers and sponsors that we had to drop the event and asking if anyone would like to pick it up for us. People started asking us more questions about what that would entail. We talked about the time and expense it took for us to put it on versus the payback we received. We stressed how much we loved the event, how much we loved the people who came to the event (who came only to play golf), and how we wished we could continue the event.

What little resistance we got came from the handful of people whose only financial support to Generations Group Homes came from buying a ticket for the golf day.

The more we talked with our volunteers and golfers, the more people realized that, as a nonprofit organization, we just couldn't be spending so much time putting on a nice day of golf for everyone. We also realized that we had a strong group of volunteers who were a great help on the day of the event, but they did not have the time or energy to put into the planning and execution of the event.

A few months into this process, we were doing a Point of Entry at our children's home for a group of Rotarians. We got to talking about their annual charity golf tournament, the proceeds of which had been given to another organization that had only wanted to show up and take the check. The Rotarians heard us talking about our support system of great volunteers for the day of the event, and, of course, the passion for our mission. A week later, we received a call from the Rotary Club saying they were naming us full recipient of their tournament's proceeds. We said a big thank you, sent out information about this new tournament to all of our past golfers, signed up our volunteers to help work the day of their tournament, and even had our executive director and board chair there at the awards dinner to say a few words about Generations Group Homes and to pick up the check. What a win-win!

So, don't be afraid to "bless and release" even a long-standing event. You won't know what it could lead to next until you do it.

Before you fill in the column stating by when you will eliminate these events, let's talk about setting up your annual rotation of events. Then we can come back and look at your timeline for phasing out—and perhaps even adding—some events.

ALIGNING YOUR EVENTS CORRECTLY THROUGHOUT THE YEAR

As you map out the years ahead using the Benevon Model, you must first decide when to hold your annual Ask Event. Everything else will revolve around that. The most popular times of the year for an Ask Event are the spring (April, May, and June) or the fall (October, November, and early December).

Here are some factors to consider in selecting the best time of year for your Ask Event:
- If you are already putting on a big fundraising event each year, in which month does it take place?
- If you are planning to convert or phase out that event, would it open up that time slot in your calendar for an Ask Event?
- If you were starting fresh, with no prior events to consider at all, when would be the ideal time to hold your Ask Event? What works best in the day-to-day life of your organization? Consider your existing annual calendar. For example, if your organization is a school, you might want to have the Ask Event in the spring, after you have been able to do Point of Entry Events starting in the fall of the prior year.

Sample Event Calendars

Nonprofit #1
- Three Point of Entry Events per month (including one Point of Entry in a Box per month).
- One Ask Event per year in the spring.
- Two Free Feel-Good Cultivation Events per year:
  ▴ One Free Feel-Good Cultivation Event in August on a private boat.
  ▴ One Free Feel-Good Cultivation Event at year-end holidays: donor recognition with kids singing, testimonials, Visionary Leader Talk.
- Zero Point of Entry Conversion Events.

Nonprofit #2
- Three Point of Entry Events per month (including one Point of Entry in a Box per month).
- One Ask Event per year in the fall.
- Three Free Feel-Good Cultivation Events per year for donors:
  ▴ One Free Feel-Good Cultivation Event in January: a private dinner for the top two levels of Multiple-Year Giving Society Donors.

- ▲ One Free Feel-Good Cultivation Event in June for all Multiple-Year Giving Society Donors: a donor/volunteer recognition dinner or annual meeting with awards and a big name speaker in the field related to the group's work.
- ▲ One Free Feel-Good Cultivation Event for all donors.
- One Point of Entry Conversion Event in March: corporate banquet—board chair's firm underwrites meal cost. Other corporations pay $10,000 to host tables; nets $100,000; ten-minute program while everyone is seated; Visionary Leader Talk, Testimonial Speaker; business cards given to table host if guest wants more information.

Let's look at an example of a Christian school that was starting out with a long list of events, but decided to design the most efficient System of Events. How could they best convert, rotate, eliminate, or add events over time to build the best possible system?

Looking down the left events column on their System of Events chart on the next page, the golf outing and gala/auction were not directly mission-based. They took an enormous amount of time to produce. They were the obvious candidates for conversion or elimination.

The remaining program-related events they were already putting on, like the graduation, volunteer-recognition event, chess classes, tutoring sessions, and the occasional drop-by one-on-one tours, were all mission-based and could easily be folded into their regular Point of Entry Events or underwritten by a donor or sponsor and converted to Free Feel-Good Cultivation Events.

DESIGNING YOUR SYSTEM OF EVENTS 125

SYSTEM OF EVENTS

Current Events	Convert Event To:						Ideal Month	Add/Convert/Eliminate By When
	Pre-Point of Entry Event	Point of Entry Event	Point of Entry in a Box	One-on-One Point of Entry	Point of Entry Conversion Event	Free Feel-Good Cultivation Event		
1. Golf outing								Eliminate now
2. Corporate-sponsored gala/auction					X		March	Convert year 1; Eliminate year 2
3. Graduation						X	June	This year
4. Chess classes		Tour stop					Monthly	Now
5. Tutoring sessions		Tour stop					Monthly	Now
6. Holiday open house				X			December	This year
7. Volunteer recognition						X	April	This year
8. Occasional school tours		X					Monthly	Now
9. Speaking to Rotary clubs, realtors' associations	X						As requested	
10. Ask Event							November	This year
11. Private dinner for top-level Multiple-Year Giving Society Donors					X		February	This year

Phasing Out an Event

The biggest challenge for this school was how and when to phase out the golf and gala. Because the golf outing had only happened once, there was less attachment to keeping it on the list. Many of the same volunteers who had been involved in putting it on were now part of implementing the Benevon Model, so they saw the need to "bless and release" it immediately.

The gala and auction event was another matter. It had been the main fundraiser for the school, netting over $200,000 a year for the past five years, with about 400 people in attendance each year. Clearly, it would need to be phased out more gradually, if at all. The first thing the school's Sustainable Funding Team did was an analysis of the financial results of the event. What was the breakdown of where that $200,000 net proceeds came from? First they noted the gross amount raised at the event, which was nearly $400,000. Over 80% of that came from the corporate sponsors who bought tables at the event. The remaining 20% came from the proceeds of the live and silent auctions. Upon further analysis of the auction results, they learned that the silent auction barely broke even, before they even accounted for all the work of the volunteers to put together the auction packages and baskets and day-of-event logistics. The live auction had been productive, but only due to three big items. Interestingly, the biggest ticket item had been their "fund-a-need" item (similar to the "fund-a-child" auction from the food bank example mentioned earlier), where every guest could "win" by raising their bid paddle to contribute to the school's tuition-assistance fund. Over half of the live auction proceeds went to that one item alone.

They decided to make a plan and give themselves a deadline. They would do two more auction events—at the most. Just making that bold decision set their minds working with creative alternatives. One of the board members—who, along with her husband, had chaired the big event last year—offered to talk with each corporate sponsor individually to tell them their decision to phase out the event, due to the high costs of putting it on. She told them about the new more mission-centered approach that the school had adopted and invited them to sit at one of the tables she and her husband would be hosting at the Ask Event, so they could see firsthand this new approach. She thanked them sincerely for being one of the very early supporters of the school and said she would be back in touch to ask them to get involved in this new effort.

Another member of the Sustainable Funding Team agreed to focus on all the auction guests who had contributed to the tuition-assistance "fund-a-need" item. There were over 100 people who had done that. Working with the development director, this team member planned a Free Feel-Good Cultivation Event at the school for all of these donors. The program included a brief talk from the board member who chaired the tuition-assistance committee, along with a single father and a grandmother who each talked about what those dollars had meant for them and their children. The program ended with one of the students speaking about the values she had learned at the school that she would carry with her for the rest of her life.

Donors who could not attend this fabulous Free Feel-Good Cultivation Event received personal letters from the students who had received tuition assistance and an invitation to the upcoming graduation ceremony.

Each donor received a Follow-Up Call to ask for their feedback and if they might like to become more involved. Those who said yes were invited to become Table Captains at the upcoming first Ask Event. They were invited to attend a Point of Entry tour in the next month or two, allowing enough time for them to invite other friends (including others who had sat at their tables at the auction gala) to subsequent Point of Entry Events, in hopes that some of them would also choose to become more involved and come to the Ask Event.

In fact, the Sustainable Funding Team made a point of seeing that everyone who had given to that mission-focused auction item received a personal telephone invitation to the Ask Event from someone on the auction committee, inviting them to sit at a VIP table with other auction donors.

By following the model beautifully, and by incorporating this conversion strategy, the school's first Ask Event netted over $350,000, including nearly $75,000 in a pooled sponsorship from three companies that had been auction sponsors.

It ended up taking the school only one more year of the auction gala before they were able to phase it out altogether. Many of those original donors of the "fund-a-need" tuition-assistance auction item are now Multiple-Year Giving Society Donors and have since become Table Captains at subsequent Ask Events, constantly introducing new people to the school.

I hope that this example demonstrates the level of creative thinking and customization that is necessary as you go about converting events. There is no one-size-fits-all approach to doing this. Which events are you considering eliminating or phasing out? Start by going right to the financial analysis of your event. Where does it make money, and where does it lose money? Then figure out which volunteers or staff members need to be converted in the process—this is clearly not just about the money! Who is the best person to talk with each of them, sensitively, to thank them sincerely for their past work and to engage them in the transition process so they can feel a sense of ownership in your plan to build sustainable funding?

ADDING EVENTS—FILLING IN THE MISSING PIECES

After re-categorizing each existing event, the team from this school was able to stand back, hold up this event chart against the ideal System of Events that they were aiming for, and easily see that they were still missing two events: an Ask Event and one Free Feel-Good Cultivation Event for the highest level donors in their Multiple-Year Giving Society. Is your organization missing any events that you need to add?

Looking at the Sample System of Events chart on page 125, the column on the far right, stating the month in which the event will take place each year, you can see that the school decided to put its new Ask Event in November. They made that decision by process of elimination—they already had so many events in the spring, that they had to put the Ask Event in the fall. But that posed other problems. Knowing some of our formulas for filling their Ask Event with enough people who had been to a prior Point of Entry and been well cultivated, would mean getting started with their Point of Entry Events during the prior school year and having them take place over the summer months as well.

As much work as they knew it would take to put a whole new system in place so quickly, they rose to the challenge. They knew that even if they had to start with a smaller first Ask Event, they needed to get the process going. Committing to a date for their first Ask Event pulled everyone forward. Working backwards from that date, they could plot out on the calendar exactly what had to be done and when. They identified many opportunities already in their school calendar for inviting people to their new Point of Entry Events, like their spring volunteer recognition event. They started talking up the process—as opposed to talking up just the Ask Event—at board meetings, hosting a special "kick-the-tires" Point of Entry just for the board. This inspired several board members to join their Sustainable Funding Team and get more training in the Benevon Model so they could be more effective internal champions moving forward.

Just as a "what-if," let's say the school had decided not to phase out the auction gala event. Perhaps there were some real skeptics on the board who were not willing to "bless and release" that event so quickly, despite the financial analysis. How else could the internal champions for the model have gotten started with the model? One option is with a smaller, high-end Ask Event.

We had one group that was really cynical about changing their outdated ways. Their CEO, who had also been their founder many years before, had come to our workshops back in the early days before we required a whole team of people to attend together. The CEO knew that he would be retiring soon, and he saw the model as a pathway to financial sustainability for his program. Excited as he was, he could not budge another soul on the board to even consider trying something other than their annual holiday appeal letter, which yielded about $100,000. As part of their coaching package that comes with our workshops, we did a conference call with their board. Somehow, miracle of miracles, we were able to persuade the majority of the board to just attend the Ask Event, without having to do anything prior to it to invite people to Point of Entry Events, fill tables, etc.

The CEO told the board, "We're going to start this in a small way. I know you are skeptical about how this will work for us." All he asked of them was, "Just show up." He told them, "We will have two special VIP tables for you to sit at."

One of the board members generously agreed to donate the venue: the private club where he was a member. Because the organization's mission was terrific and because they followed the model, their Point of Entry Events were very successful. They had no problem finding enough passionate Table Captains to fill the room with fifty people who were "ripened fruit." Sure enough, they exceeded our standard formula for Ask Event results, raising over $100,000, and adding eight first-time members to their Multiple-Year Giving Society (for gifts of $1,000 a year or more for each of the next five years).

Of course, because the event was so good, some of the skeptical board members were moved to tears, reconnected to why they joined the board so many years ago, and many of them gave generously as well. At the next board meeting, they voted to adopt the model wholeheartedly and to use it to build toward sustainable funding. We were able to help them launch an endowment and get a planned giving program in place. Now, nearly 100% of their board members are long-term donors to that program.

Sometimes it takes that dogged determination and the willingness to start small to get the model going in an organization.

IT'S STILL A LOT TO DO

Once you finish designing your System of Events, even after it is pared back to the basics, you can see that you still have a lot of events to choreograph each year: monthly Point of Entry Events, one Ask Event per year, and two or three Free Feel-Good Cultivation Events—that adds up to at least fifteen to sixteen "events" a year. While many of the Point of Entry Events will replace other tours and program events you may already do, there is still a good deal of work needed to polish them up and get them ready for outsiders to view on a regular basis.

Some words of encouragement: weeding out your most labor-intensive events will be the hardest part. But once you create your annual System of Events, inserting your mission into every event, the entire quality of your events will shift. People will call you after the events to see how they can become involved. Rather than having your staff's limited time be bogged down in planning the next event, your staff and volunteers will be ready and available to take those calls and stay with those donors through the cultivation process. In other words, it won't take many "missionized" events before the work of your existing staff can shift from putting on special events to the key pathway to sustainable funding—major gifts cultivation and asking.

Before we tie the final ribbon and bow on your new System of Events, let's look at two more special scenarios: milestone and holiday events.

CHAPTER 12

MILESTONE EVENTS

It's your organization's twenty-fifth anniversary, your founder or CEO is retiring after twenty-two years, you are moving into your new office building, or your organization or one of your top researchers just won a cherished award in your field. These are major milestones. And, like the birth of a child, a graduation ceremony, or a wedding, these milestones deserve to be celebrated.

What is the best way to celebrate these key occasions, while also linking people to your organization's mission? Let's look at three examples.

ORGANIZATION'S ANNIVERSARY

While not everyone in the community will agree that this is worth putting on a tuxedo or evening gown to celebrate, it is a milestone event in the life of your organization and worthy of publicity and some hoopla. Think through what you intend to accomplish over the days, months, or year of the anniversary. Is your main agenda fundraising, bringing back longtime (and often lost) supporters, engaging new people, or all of the above?

What is the overall theme of the celebration? For example, if it's your tenth anniversary, the theme may be pioneers, honoring those who made these first ten years possible. If it is your twenty-fifth anniversary, you might have a founders theme, quarter-of-a-century theme, or heroes theme.

How many events or occasions do you want to have? How can you convert them into one of your existing Benevon events, like your Point of Entry Events, Ask Event, or Free Feel-Good Cultivation Events? Is this the time to announce the launch of a capital or endowment campaign?

If you have been using the model successfully over time, you should have a ready supply of committed mission-focused donors who will be delighted to participate in your events or support your campaign. Just be sure to keep it all mission-focused—don't get sidetracked into entertaining people as your sole purpose.

A big anniversary can be a wonderful opportunity to bring in an important speaker on your topic: a top researcher in your field or a celebrity champion of your cause. It's a great time to have a little fun, maybe even poke fun at yourselves. Insert a Point of Entry element into each occasion, giving people some myth-buster facts about your accomplishments and a wonderful Visionary Leader Talk about the past, present, and exciting future ahead. Share some engaging insider anecdotes and testimonials so that people remember the way your work changes lives every day. And remember, unless it's an Ask Event, don't ask for money.

RETIREMENT OF FOUNDER OR EXECUTIVE DIRECTOR

This is a great opportunity for a special fundraising effort or campaign. Regardless of people's sentiments about the person who is retiring, they will want to honor the person and/or celebrate the entrance of the new person. (Of course, since you have been using the model for awhile, you know that the real allegiance of your supporters is to your mission, not to any one individual.)

Here is a suggested scenario:

At an Ask Event one year prior to your CEO's actual retirement (assuming the news of the retirement can be announced this far in advance), announce the retirement and say something like, "Our CEO (or founder), Marlene, would like nothing more than to leave here knowing that our funding is secured into the future. You will be hearing more about a special endowment fund we are setting up in honor of Marlene's twenty-seven years of service, called the Legacy Fund."

After the Ask Event, have some of your Multiple-Year Giving Society Donors host private Point of Re-Entry Events for these existing donors in their homes or offices to talk about the new endowment fund and share your dream of reaching $5 million before Marlene's retirement next year. Then follow up individually, answering their questions and continuing to cultivate these donors one-on-one, until they are ready to be asked to give.

At Marlene's retirement banquet a year later, you can announce the amount raised for the Legacy Fund and perhaps have some of the new donors speak about why they chose to fund it—to carry on Marlene's legacy.

MOVING INTO A NEW BUILDING

This is a wonderful opportunity for a series of recognition and celebration events, as well as Point of Entry Events to introduce new people to your organization. Think (in advance) of all the people who need to be recognized at this event—everyone from the contractor to the company that donated the new air-conditioning unit. If the building has been financed or paid for with the help of a capital campaign, those are the donors to honor at the move-in celebration. You may want to have a private move-in event, just for the inner circle of high-end donors, for you to recognize them in a smaller group first. You may also put on a bigger acknowledgment event for the entire community. The scope of the project will help you determine the scope of the recognition.

Do not overlook your Multiple-Year Giving Society Donors who give to support your unrestricted operational needs. You can schedule special, donor-only tours, which also serve as Point of Re-Entry Events, and you should encourage them to bring friends. Insert a Visionary Leader Talk and a testimonial to remind them what their ongoing support has allowed you to do over these years. Cite statistics about the rate of growth, numbers served, and how their ongoing multiple-year support gave you the financial stability and confidence to build the new home for your organization. Honor the role they played in getting you to this place. And remember that many of the Multiple-Year Giving Society Donors—if cultivated properly over time—will become excellent candidates for future campaigns.

Let's turn now to holiday events.

CHAPTER 13

MAKING THE MOST OF THE HOLIDAY SEASON

The holidays are open season for events. Now that you understand how to missionize each event, let's step back and see how to seamlessly weave these holiday occasions into your System of Events.

WHAT MAKES THE HOLIDAY SEASON UNIQUE?

The holiday season is special, first, because it is a time when people naturally connect with one another. We all get more invitations to attend social functions—whether for business, personal, or charitable events. More people are talking to each other. Whether in person beside the punchbowl at a holiday party or by mail, phone, or e-mail, this is a season of natural communication. This is a ripe opportunity for people to be talking about their association with your organization.

Second, the holiday season is the one time of year when we are genuinely encouraged to be kind, generous, and caring toward others. People expect others to be doing good deeds during the holidays. We take extra pleasure in helping others at this time of year. Faith groups, employee groups, and families are all looking for projects to take on that demonstrate their compassion for others. People give time and in-kind goods: food baskets, toys, and time to listen to others. It's a natural season for people to express their goodwill.

Third, this is a season of giving money. Punctuated by the end of the tax year, people are taking stock of how they have fared financially, and many choose to make financial contributions now. The first organizations they will give to will be those they have remained most loyal to over the years—their "default charities." These are the organizations they feel connected to emotionally. There is no question about giving to these places. Next are the organizations they may have become involved with more recently. In those final weeks and months of the year, which "new" organizations will they give to? What will those fortunate organizations have done throughout the year to position their envelope in the "yes" stack of mail? Again, knowing that the majority of giving is done at year-end should be helpful information for your organization.

WHERE WILL YOU FOCUS?

The great temptation for most nonprofit organizations at the end of the year is to focus solely on asking for and receiving money. Think of the time and energy spent on this within your organization: mailings, phone-a-thons, and one-on-one Asks. If the cultivation work has been done throughout the year, this is a season of much asking and much giving. It is time: your organization definitely needs to focus on picking the fruit.

However, in the frenzy of sending out holiday solicitation mailings and other year-end activities, the rich opportunities for connecting with people during this season are often overlooked. If you can broaden your organization's reach over the holidays to include those people who may be meeting you for the first time or reconnecting after a lapse of time, you will see many opportunities for deepening the connection and building lifelong donors.

What if you could use each occasion during the holidays strategically as a full-scale or mini-Point of Entry or Point of Re-Entry? Rather than having to go to the work of attracting people to your mid-year Point of Entry Events, what if you could take advantage of the already-established gatherings to tell or update people about the work of your organization?

Further, imagine that all of your volunteers and board members were well-trained and deputized to be walking One-on-One Point of Entry Events wherever they go throughout the holiday season. Imagine the seeds that would be planted or fruit that would be further ripened, ready for picking in the next year.

Your goal with these holiday Point of Entry Events is to make an indelible impression about the essential work of your organization. If this is their first contact, each visitor or guest should leave inspired and stirred up about your outstanding programs. If this is not their first contact, they should have been powerfully reconnected to your mission and acknowledged for their support. In any case, they should be looking forward to talking with you further in the New Year. They should be launched and on their way to becoming a lifelong donor.

HOLIDAY POINT OF ENTRY EVENTS: THE MESSAGE

Whether you will be planning group or One-on-One Point of Entry Events, Point of Re-Entry Events, or converting existing holiday events into Point of Entry Conversion Events, there are two things to keep in mind at the holiday season. First, your guests will be busier than ever. Second, they want to be inspired and to make a difference.

Conveying your message in a clear, concise, inspiring way that will stand out amongst all the other holiday messages takes some careful planning. The place to start is with your well-honed Point of Entry in a Box format that has been tested over time. Then you can tweak it a bit for the holidays.

Making Your Needs Clear

More than ever, during the holidays you must make the needs of your organization clear. This does not mean you will be asking for anything specifically at a Point of Entry, but rather that you are making it clear to people that their involvement with your organization is needed year-round and would make a huge difference in their lives and in the lives of the people you serve.

Sprucing Up Your Point of Entry Materials

Before we consider the many permutations of holiday Point of Entry and Point of Re-Entry Events, let's be sure your basic Point of Entry materials are ready for the season. Just as you add candles or special photographs and flowers to your room decor at holiday time, it is a good idea to warm up your printed Point of Entry materials as well.

Fact Sheet

While the points to be made remain the same, you can certainly spin them a bit for the holidays. You may want to include seasonal trends, such as the number of elderly people in nursing homes with no family who visit them during the holidays, or the number of concert tickets your orchestra donates to school children and families over the holidays.

You may want to make new pie charts that highlight or summarize the percentage of your annual goals that have been achieved or remain to be reached. Do not underestimate the power of the Fact Sheet. Emotion alone won't build your organization loyal lifelong donors. They have got to understand and be hooked by the facts as well.

Wish List

Be sure your Wish List is ready for the holidays. Remove any items you have already received and update the list with new items. Ask each program or department to list their top five needs. Have them be as specific as possible: large and small items, pots and pans, diapers, computers, gas for the van, or a new music instructor or counselor.

Then compile them all into a single Wish List. You might consider listing them by area or department: "The nursery is wishing for diapers. The maintenance staff is wishing for gas for the van." It will let people know that you really need these items.

Print them up on holiday-type paper. Make enough copies so that you can distribute them generously throughout the season. Have them at your front door or at the reception desk for visitors to take. Insert them in your newsletter. Have a little basket of them at your holiday parties and other events.

Your Holiday Point of Entry Opportunities

Look at your organization's calendar of events and activities that could become holiday Point of Entry Events. Include, for example, open houses, recognition events, and volunteer group projects. Do not overlook the many program-related events like student music concerts or unscheduled alumni visits that tend to crop up over the holidays.

What if every event you produced this holiday season, from bake sales to black-tie galas, were treated like a Point of Entry or a Point of Re-Entry? Use the opportunity of having all these folks gathered together to educate and inspire them about your programs and services.

Think about how you could use the holiday season to enhance your System of Events, including your:
- Point of Entry Events
- One-on-One Point of Entry Events
- Point of Entry Conversion Events
- Free Feel-Good Cultivation Events (or Point of Re-Entry Events)

YEAR-END POINT OF ENTRY EVENTS

You will definitely want to keep your regularly scheduled year-round Point of Entry Events going during the holiday season—just be sure to plan the dates of your holiday season Point of Entry Events strategically. Plot out on a calendar when your other holiday events and mailings are happening. When do the bulk of your pre-holiday inquiry calls come in? Is there a rush of calls in conjunction with your holiday open house or some other event? Time your Point of Entry Events accordingly. I recommend planning one Point of Entry for the month of November, one in early December, and one for January. That way, as people are calling in to inquire about other events or projects, your staff or volunteers can be inviting them to Point of Entry Events.

Most groups find they have more guests at these year-end Point of Entry Events. Whereas during the rest of the year, your volunteers and staff will be reaching out to people and inviting them to come and learn more about your organization, the holiday season should naturally generate a larger list of guests—people who are calling you to inquire about volunteer projects, articles they read about your needs, and ways to give in-kind gifts. From there, you can sort out where they can best be accommodated and invite them to a Point of Entry Event.

Many organizations use the Point of Entry as a starting point to sort and refer the many groups that may approach them with projects over the holidays. For example, an employee work group had assigned one man the job of checking out several holiday project volunteer opportunities. The group selected a project, but the man was so inspired by the Point of Entry of one of the other organizations that he became personally involved with that organization and brought in a different volunteer group that he was a part of.

ONE-ON-ONE POINT OF ENTRY EVENTS

The holiday season presents innumerable opportunities for One-on-One Point of Entry Events, if you and your team are tuned into them—whether at formal holiday events sponsored by your organization or when your board, volunteers, and other supporters are attending their own social events throughout the holiday season. The key, of course, is being aware of these mini-opportunities and being prepared to take advantage of them.

Recalling the format for the One-on-One Point of Entry discussed in Chapter 6, be sure that your team has practiced their "script" and can cover all of the points in the context of a brief, easy-flowing conversation.

The goal in these brief conversations is to cover enough material so that the person ends up saying, naturally, as you part: "Let's get together to talk more about that after the holidays."

POINT OF ENTRY CONVERSION EVENTS

How could you easily convert the many holiday community-group presentations you already have scheduled into Point of Entry Conversion or Pre-Point of Entry Events? What about all of the corporate employee groups who call in wanting to take on a project for you over the holidays—taking a holiday dinner to a shut-in elderly person or having a class of school kids to serve dinner at your homeless shelter? How could you insert your mission and capture the names (with permission) of the people who want to learn more?

What if your organization does not have direct service opportunities for volunteers? How can you create volunteer opportunities that will be attractive to groups at this time of year? This approach is not just limited to human services organizations serving children and families in need. Arts, environmental, advocacy, and even membership organizations need ready projects that community groups can take on. What bite-sized chunk of your programs or services could they adopt or sponsor? Cleaning up a roadway, park, or trail; helping with a year-end letter writing campaign to legislators; or even helping to paint or clean an office can be satisfying, self-contained volunteer projects for eager groups at year-end. Your organization needs to be ready to publicize such opportunities in the summer and fall when faith-based and employee groups are selecting their year-end community service projects. Then your challenge is to convert these project-centered volunteer experiences into bona fide Point of Entry Conversion Events or to attach them on a Point of Entry in a Box. In either case, they must include the three essential ingredients of a Point of Entry.

Capturing the Names with Permission

This is usually quite simple at a Point of Entry Conversion Event like a volunteer workday. Just have a sign-in table with a card for each person to complete with their name, address, phone number, and e-mail. You can have a box on the sign-in card for people to check off if they would like to receive more information about your organization. People will expect to have to sign in as part of standard volunteer procedure within your organization. Furthermore, depending on the type of work they will be doing, you may have legal waivers of liability for them to sign. Handle all that at the beginning, then ask them to take a seat for a brief orientation about the day's project, which is where you can insert your Point of Entry elements.

FREE FEEL-GOOD CULTIVATION EVENTS

Which events and activities that you already have scheduled over the holidays could become Free Feel-Good Cultivation Events? Consider the special recognition events for donors, board, volunteers, or staff, student holiday performances, candlelight vigils, etc. Now that you are aware of the opportunity to insert a brief program element to update, inspire, and re-connect prior supporters and friends with your current work, as well as educate their friends for the first time, how could you do that? Knowing that this event is scheduled to happen anyway, how could you expand its reach by inviting targeted sub-groups of donors or potential donors?

Since the majority of the guests will be current or prior supporters, these events are an ideal opportunity to set the stage for everything you want to have happen next year. You have plenty of permission to share with them your accomplishments of the year that is ending, as well as your dreams for next year and beyond. Now is the time to let them know if you are planning to launch a capital campaign, put together a matching gift Challenge Fund, or finally get that new program started. After all, as they are your insider group of supporters, it would be natural to share your plans with them early on in the process.

A WEALTH OF OPPORTUNITIES

As you begin to recognize the holiday season for the rich Point of Entry opportunities it provides, you will see more and more ways to missionize every holiday occasion, even those where you are unable to capture names with permission. Here are some other examples:

- At the annual staff party, invite one or more satisfied families or clients to come back and speak about the difference the organization made in their lives. Be sure to acknowledge the families of the staff members for the support they have provided all year.

- Send a staff speaker with a copy of your video to make lunch presentations to all those community groups who want to "Adopt a Family" or "Adopt a Child" for the holidays. Make sure they know the year-round needs of that family or child and how they can keep contributing.
- At the annual volunteer or board recognition, give out awards that highlight the one-on-one impact of your work. If you are an arts organization, have a child or parent speak about what the theater or ballet has meant to your child. Use it as an opportunity to thank those who contributed the funds that enabled you to offer those free or discounted tickets. Showcase the volunteers who went the extra mile. Let them, or someone who benefited, tell how it changed their lives.
- At your bake sale or holiday fair, find a way to tell people what your organization does. Station an articulate, passionate staff member at a booth near the front door. Or have the focus of the fair be on the accomplishments of your entrepreneurial, artistic, or high-tech urban kids.

THE BOTTOM LINE

The holidays are high season for events. It is the time of year when people are naturally connecting with each other, are open to caring and making a difference, and want to hear those sentimental stories about how lives were changed. You don't have to stretch the truth or parade any "poster children." Just tell them the facts and share a firsthand story or testimonial. If you plan for the holiday season with the Benevon Model in mind, you will see innumerable opportunities for missionizing every event.

CHAPTER 14

MOVING FORWARD

As you move forward with your newly crafted System of Events, I hope you will take pride in knowing that, merely by shifting your thinking, you have begun a process of restoring your organization's cherished mission as the centerpiece of your fundraising activities. Never again will you be content to spend the limited resources of your organization planning an old-style, "entertainment-only" fundraising event. Rather, you will infuse each event with a Point of Entry program element to educate and inspire people and connect or reconnect them to your great work.

Then, using our systematic process for donor development, you will systematically follow up, cultivate, and ask donors for significant multiple-year pledges for unrestricted operating funds. Over time, many of these same donors will "self-cultivate," deepening their involvement with your organization at their own choosing. Some will be capable of making larger gifts for operating funds, capital needs, and ultimately endowment.

In those same precious hours you are now spending planning events, you will be meeting with individual donors, listening to their hopes and dreams for your organization, talking about how "we" can fulfill those dreams together. You will have given those donors the opportunity to do so much more than enjoy a nice event—you will have allowed them to make a true contribution to the lasting—sustainable—legacy of an organization whose mission is their mission too.

APPENDIX

VISIONARY LEADER TALK WORKSHEET

Name of organization: _____

I. Your personal story (one minute)
   A. What personal incident or experience in your life brought you to this organization in the first place? _____
   _____

   B. What keeps you working there? _____
   _____

II. Mission/history of the organization (one minute)
   A. When was it founded? _____
      By whom? _____
   B. Why does the organization really exist? _____
   _____

   C. What values does it teach, encourage, or represent? _____
   _____

   D. How has it evolved and grown since the beginning? _____
   _____

III. The gap (two minutes)
   A. How many people are unserved or underserved now? _____
   B. What is the personal impact of the absence of those needed programs and services on each guest's life? _____
   _____

IV. Vision for the future (two minutes)
   A. What will it take for you to fulfill your mission? _____
   _____

   B. Where do you want to be five to ten years from now? _____
   _____

   C. If you accomplish your goals, what will be the impact on the broader community? _____
   _____

ABOUT THE AUTHOR

Terry Axelrod is the founder and CEO of Benevon (formerly Raising More Money), which trains and coaches nonprofit organizations to implement a mission-based system for raising sustainable funding from individual donors. This system ends the suffering about fundraising and builds passionate and committed lifelong donors.

With nearly forty years of experience in the nonprofit field, Axelrod has founded three nonprofits in the fields of health care and affordable housing. She realized early in her career that the only path to sustainable funding was to systematically connect donors to the mission of the organization, then involve and cultivate them until they were clearly ready to give—in short, to treat donors the way you would treat a close friend or family member, someone with whom you planned to have a lifelong relationship.

Axelrod created the Benevon Model in 1996 after serving as development consultant to Zion Preparatory Academy, an inner-city Christian academy in Seattle, from 1992–1995. There she designed and implemented fundraising and marketing programs which yielded $7.2 million in two-and-a-half years as well as national recognition of the program, including a cover story in *The Chronicle of Philanthropy.*

Author of five other books, *Raising More Money—A Step-by-Step Guide to Building Lifelong Donors, Raising More Money—The Point of Entry Handbook, Raising More Money—The Ask Event Handbook, Beyond the Ask Event,* and *The Joy of Fundraising,* Axelrod is also a sought-after speaker, both nationally and internationally. Her passionate commitment to the possibility of sustainable funding for all nonprofits drives the mission of Benevon and each of its programs. "The donors are truly out there—wanting to contribute; it's up to the organizations to connect donors powerfully to their work and nurture that connection over time. Our programs give each organization the tools to do that successfully."

Axelrod currently serves as a Life Trustee of Swedish Medical Center. She received her Master's of Social Work and Bachelor's Degrees at the University of Michigan, and she resides in Seattle with her husband, Alan, and their two children.

ADDITIONAL INFORMATION AND RESOURCES

Visit our Web site at www.benevon.com to:
- Subscribe to our free bi-weekly electronic newsletter, the Benevon E-New$.
- Register for one of our many free or inexpensive introductory sessions.
- Register for our Curriculum for Sustainable Funding.
- Purchase books and DVDs about Benevon.
- Learn about the Benevon Next Step donor-tracking system.
- Browse the Benevon archives for additional information on building sustainable funding from lifelong individual donors.

INDEX

Appreciation *see* Free Feel-Good Cultivation Events
Ask Event *see* Free One-Hour Ask Event
Asking
    Asking for money, 14-18, 24-26, 71-82
    One-on-One Asking, 15-16, 86
    see also Free One-Hour Ask Event; Pitch

Benevon Model
    Step One: Point of Entry *see* Point of Entry Events
    Step Two: Follow Up and Involve *see* Cultivation Superhighway; Follow-up; Follow-Up Calls
    Step Three: Asking for Money *see* Asking; Free One-Hour Ask Event
    Step Four: Donors Introducing Others *see* Free Feel-Good Cultivation Events
"Bless and release," 12-13, 120-122
Brochure *see* Handouts at the Point of Entry

Capital campaigns, 20, 27, 85, 144
Capture the names, 9, 107, 144
Challenge Gift, 87
Contacts *see* Cultivation Superhighway
Contribution *see* Asking
Conversion Events *see* Point of Entry Conversion Events
Cultivation *see* Cultivation Superhighway; Follow-up; Follow-Up Calls; Free Feel-Good Cultivation Events

Cultivation Superhighway, 13-16
   see also Follow-up; Follow-Up Calls
Customization *see* Cultivation Superhighway

Donation *see* Asking
Donors
   Cultivation *see* Cultivation Superhighway
   Multiple-Year Giving Society Donors *see* Multiple-Year Giving Society
   Recognition of *see* Free Feel-Good Cultivation Events

Emotional Hook, 8, 25-27, 75-76
   see also Essential Story
Endowment, 5-6, 20, 27, 85
Essential Story, 47-50, 67
   see also Emotional Hook
Events
   Phasing out existing events, 28, 31, 96, 120-123, 126-129
   see also Free Feel-Good Cultivation Events; Free One-Hour Ask Event; Point of Entry Conversion Events; Point of Entry Events; System of Events

Fact Sheet *see* Handouts at the Point of Entry
Feedback *see* Follow-up
Follow-up
   Calls *see* Follow-Up Calls
   Step Two: Follow Up and Involve, 10-13, 107, 109-115
   see also Cultivation Superhighway

Follow-Up Calls, 10-12, 19, 109, 112-113
  Permission for *see* Capture the names
  see also Cultivation Superhighway
Free Feel-Good Cultivation Events, 19-20, 26-28, 83-93, 144
Free One-Hour Ask Event, 16, 24-26, 71-82

Giving levels *see* Units of Service

Handouts at the Point of Entry
  Basic brochure, 53
  Fact Sheet, 53, 140
  Wish List, 53, 140
Hook *see* Emotional Hook

Introducing others *see* Free Feel-Good Cultivation Events

Legacy, 117, 147
Levels of giving *see* Units of Service
Lifelong donor *see* Donors; Multiple-Year Giving Society

Model for raising money *see* Benevon Model
Money *see* Asking; Pitch
Multiple-Year Giving Society, 16-20, 28, 72-74, 83, 90, 135
Myth-buster facts, 47, 66

Names, capturing *see* Capture the names

One-Hour Ask Event *see* Asking; Free One-Hour Ask Event
One-on-one asking *see* Asking

Permission *see* Capture the names
Personal contacts *see* Cultivation Superhighway
Phasing out existing events *see* Events
Pitch, 72, 79
Pitch Person, 79
Planning events *see* System of Events
Pledges, 16-18, 72-73, 79
Point of Entry Conversion Events, 28-30, 95-107
Point of Entry Events
    Agenda, 43
    Guests referring others, 12, 22, 42, 55
    Timing, 53-54
    Venue, 51-52
    see also Emotional Hook; Handouts at the Point of Entry;
        Testimonials; Visionary Leader
Point of Re-Entry Events *see* Free Feel-Good Cultivation Events

Recognition *see* Free Feel-Good Cultivation Events
Re-Entry Events *see* Free Feel-Good Cultivation Events

Steps in Benevon Model
    Step One: Point of Entry *see* Point of Entry Events
    Step Two: Follow Up and Involve *see* Cultivation
        Superhighway; Follow-up; Follow-Up Calls

Step Three: Asking for Money *see* Asking; Free One-Hour
Ask Event
Step Four: Donors Introducing Others *see* Free Feel-Good
Cultivation Events
System of Events, 30-32, 117-131

Table Captains, 74, 79-81
Testimonials, 50, 52, 78-79
Tracking system, 11, 67, 113

Units of Service, 17-18

Video, 77-78
Visionary Leader, 45-46, 77, 87, 149
Volunteers, 15, 57-58, 141-143, 145

Wish List *see* Handouts at the Point of Entry